JUBILANT THICKET

"As earthy as a truffle and as refined
as holy water, Jonathan Williams
is a man whose tastes cross worlds."

—Rob Neufeld,
Asheville Citizen-Times, 8/29/2004

JW, Skywinding Farm, Scaly Mountain, NC, 2003
Photograph by Reuben Cox

JUBILANT THICKET

New & Selected Poems

JONATHAN WILLIAMS

COPPER CANYON PRESS

Cover art: *Cape Cod, 1972,* photograph by Harry Callahan, used with the kind permission of the Estate of Harry Callahan, PaceWildensteinMacGill, and the Aperture Foundation.

Copper Canyon Press is in residence at Fort Worden State Park in Port Townsend, Washington, under the auspices of Centrum Foundation. Centrum is a gathering place for artists and creative thinkers from around the world, students of all ages and backgrounds, and audiences seeking extraordinary cultural enrichment.

Library of Congress Cataloging-in-Publication Data

Williams, Jonathan, 1929–
  Jubilant thicket : new & selected poems / Jonathan Williams
      p. cm.
  ISBN 1-55659-202-7 (pbk. : alk. paper)
  I. Title.
  PS3545.I52966J83 2005
  811'.54–dc22
  2004020436

98765432
FIRST PRINTING

COPPER CANYON PRESS
Post Office Box 271
Port Townsend, Washington 98368
www.coppercanyonpress.org

This project took a tremendous amount of work and time at the computer. Jonathan Williams hides behind pseudo-antiquity, calls himself "Buddy Luddite," and hasn't got the savvy required. So, Tom Meyer took up the job and he deserves a lot of general thanksgiving. (JW's even afraid of the Internet—he's hardly ever looked. Says he: "I suspect it is a younger sister of the Gorgon Medusa. More than a peek or two, you might be turned into stone, or something considerably less pleasant.")

for Tom

CONTENTS

A GREETING TO THE READER   IX

I. Meta-fours   3

II. Mahler   47

III. Apple-pie Order   99
    Clerihews   101
    Limericks   109
    Acrosticals   113

IV. Scumbags from Parnassus   121

V. Bugtussle   133

VI. Nude Driver Threw Lard!   205

VII. The Flower-Hunter in the Fields   235

VIII. Homages, Elegies & Valedictions   257

ABOUT THE AUTHOR   303

A GREETING TO THE READER

At age 75 (hard for me to believe) it seems a good time to put a gom of poems on the poetry table. *Gom*'s a favorite mountain word of mine. It means "big mess of." I've been making poems for circa 55 years. *Jubilant Thicket* is a fair sample. As we know in North Carolina, where God is in charge of the barbecue, there can be "too much pork for just one fork." I asked Jim Cory, of Philadelphia, a savvy poet with a sharp eye and clear ears, to help pare it all down from 1,450 poems. I much appreciate his help.

Guy Davenport has been reading the poems since the 1960s. He assures us that all of them are "paratactic, peripatetic, and cathectic." *Cathectic* is the tough one, but let me apply it to the title, *Jubilant Thicket*. When I first saw Harry Callahan's wondrous photograph *Cape Cod, 1972*, I wanted to use it on a book of poems. In my mind (and maybe—or maybe not—in Harry's mind) I saw the bush in the sand as *Jubilant Thicket,* as pubic thatch, where much of one's poetic imagination lives and plays. Cathexis can sexualize almost anything—but not George Bush, a bush of different color.

Experience teaches me that a writer can be clearly in touch with the two generations older than himself. So, I was in love with Pound, Dr. Williams, Wallace Stevens, Cummings, Patchen, Charles Olson, Kenneth Rexroth. And one is also in touch with what writers in their fifties and sixties are up to. After that, unless you teach in universities, it all disappears. I cannot name you ten poets in their thirties. Maybe five in their twenties. These gents are very peripatetic and often ring up from Asheville or Atlanta and wish to see the hermit in his native habitat.

I started collecting records and going to concerts in 1939 (age 10), with all the offerings of Washington, DC, laid out before me. So, 65 years later, my ears don't fall off and my stomach doesn't curdle when I hear names like George Antheil, Ernest Bloch, Frank Bridge, John Corigliano, Luigi Dallapiccola, David Del Tredici, Ginastera, H.K. Gruber, Reynaldo Hahn, Charles Ives, Ligeti, E.J. Moeran, Nicolai Medtner, Conlon Nancarrow, Arvo Pärt, Einojuhani Rautavaara, Carl Ruggles, Nikos Skalkottas, Arnold Schoenberg, and Stefan Wolpe... By the time I was 20 I had been to New Orleans, Memphis, and New York—jazz and blues were added to the pot.

Back to writing, the next thing to hope for is "unabashed boys and girls" to read the stuff. This is what Basil Bunting said he dreamed of. These poems offer no grist for academic mills—many restive souls will not admit they are poems at all. But I would like to venture to say they are "monastic" and "tramontane." They have been written in the Pennine Dales and the Appalachian Mountains, and their principal cohorts have been a few good and bad Brits and Yanks, Shortia, Dog Hobble, Bluets, timber rattlers, pileated woodpeckers, rowan trees, the Greater Bell Flower, Bear Garlic, and peewits. Most of American life is quite beyond me. It's just too scary, except for the pitching of Greg Maddux. Let me quote Basil Bunting one more time—and he makes his point very clearly: "Readers are not what one writes for after one's got rid of the cruder ambitions."

The poet has tried hard to put the right words in the proper places. And to open up some of the territory ahead. Put on your walking shoes and let me take you to a lot of new places. Cheers!

JW

JUBILANT THICKET

I. META-FOURS

The poet's fascination with his dotty invention, the *meta-four*, continues. Its only "rule" is that each line have four words. All capitals and punctuation are eliminated, except for hyphens and apostrophes. The result (when it works) turns sense into nonsense and gets the mind so off-stride that you don't know whether you're coming or going. And you don't distinguish "prose" from "poetry." There is the ancient local limerick:

> *There was a young bugger from Dent,*
> *whose cock was so long that it bent.*
> *To save himself trouble,*
> *he put it in double—*
> *and instead of coming, he went!!!*

That's the idea.

Today's huckster now has about fifteen seconds in which to sell soap—thirty seconds strain the attention of the couch potato. The wastrel poet (a no-goodnik with nothing to sell to any appalled American mall-rat) may not have five seconds. He therefore alerts his words: You guys better creep in, crap, and creep out, like starting now: DO IT!

Judith Thurman gives good advice: "Start as near the end of a poem as you can."

The lines in a meta-four make sure that you do as much work as the writer did—maybe even more. Few will be willing who don't read poetry, perhaps, but the poet aspires to reach no one else—no one but *willing readers,* that is. "Cromwell, I do charge thee, Flench from ambition. By that sin fell the angels," etc.

The meta-four, like the limerick, is a form that seems to provoke a certain lubricity. There's nowt wrong with that, luv. You'll find plenty of lyricism and visionary concern later on in the book.

META-FOURS ("Voces Intimae")

courtesy of raoul middleman
so what did the
zen monk say to
the hotdog vendor make
me one with everything

a play by jardiel
pordela is titled carlo
monte in monte carlo

le artie shaw artichaut

that's it game's over
zip up your fly

estimated acres of forest
henry david thoreau burned
down in 1844 trying
to cook fish he'd
caught for dinner 300

i intended on celebrating
the supreme court sodomy
ruling by going out
and sodomizing someone last
night but my plans
fell through tra la

from nowhere a crow
came with me as
i left the city

vat 69 is not
the pope's private phoneline

ben katchor's cheap novelties
the pleasures of urban
decay featuring mr julius
knipl real estate photographer

i still remember the
classic yiddish joke ferdinand
ruge my english master
at st albans used
to tell it went
like this so what
is the difference between
the stoic and the
cynic schools of philosophy
vell de stoic is
vut brings de babies
and de cynic's vere
you vash de dishes

but egg bread is
what your mama's generation
used to call it

EAST VILLAGE BLUES
had it in my
mouth twice no dice

WE'RE EXPERIENCING AUDIO IRREGULARITIES
you do jack it
don't you peter as
big as that you
don't just sit around
and look at it

       bowflex like having an
       entire jim at home

most people over eighty
don't buy green bananas

       paulus spongopeus gistebnicenus arguably
       the most prolific bohemian
       composer of his time

     the auvergnats do rather
     elaborate things with eggs

       ecballium elaterium squirting cucumber
       discharges explosively when ripe

J.B.
what did you call
that lad who pumped
petrol at the garage
i called him angelpups
what else dumb ass
i called him angelpups

hey travis fimmel do
you still wear calvins
i wear what's clean

DYLAN
pink i likes blue
i likes but puce
i bloody hates mate

the money talks and
absolutely everybody else listens

fytp fytp fytp fytp
fuck you too pal

nc bone & joint

with all the dna
in the cum on
my stomach i could
clone myself three times

the viagra i took
with dinner stayed with
me all the way
to memphis which gave
me something to do

PEDOPHILE TV ADS ARE HERE
why do i have
aflac insurance on top
of my regular health
insurance did i say
it is because he
has his mother's thighs

yonat wiryamoso that's my
name in linear b
according to guy davenport
who should bloody know

REBUS
i'm dealing with slime
to catch a slug

a psychic and a
celebrity a camera and
a murder all come
together in this riveting
page-turner by tata bosboom

THE JOHN MURRAY ARCHIVE
it includes the pubic
hair of byron's lover

balthus smiles that on
park avenue women laugh
when they are coming

    miss charlene mason sang
    i will not pass
    this way again giving
    pleasure to the congregation
    very considerable pleasure indeed

rita was a nympho
my father knew stuff

    THOMAS WOLFE
    editing his work was
    likened to putting a
    corset on an elephant

    the name's volpo drought

    another image i embed
    my mind's eye into

AFTER OVID
jackin' the bean stalk

    where will you be
    when your diarrhea comes
    back answer me that

JACK MORTON
christ john the day
you give up smoking
is the day i
change my underwear and
that's a genuine promise

thomas jeckyll's sunflower firedogs

SCENES OF CHILDHOOD:
LAST DAY OF GENE RAMEY'S SCHOOL,
CORNELIA, GEORGIA, 1943
hurray hurray hurray hurray
the first of May
outdoor fucking starts today

father sebastian kneipp's waters

IN THE PUBLIC'S BOOK
AT R.B. KITAJ'S EXHIBITION AT THE MET
i hate this kind
of exhibit specially when
it comes from a
faget ps like him
and likewise Hockney Sam

Some Chards from Over at the Neugents' Place

well that's coon holdin'
that black snake and
back behind him that's
either frog or hell
it might be turtle
ridin' that goddamned chopper

one move you're chutney

home sweet sweaty home

O.J. in South Florida

i met this girl
once and she tells
me she only dates
guys with ten inches
i said baby i
ain't cuttin' off two
inches not for nobody

hegel once said the
owl of minerva flies
at dusk i think
i can top that
the bowel of minerva
moves at dusk so
what do you think

openly gay high school
football player visits hickory

    Bruce Boycik,
    San Diego Padres Manager
    plays by his pants
    wins with his gut

and on one climb
had his hair set
on fire by lightning

    cher maitre we brits
    are an odd lot
    some of my colleagues
    have taken to pronouncing
    your name morris ravel
    to rhyme with gravel
    the english are like
    dogs they go round
    pissing on everything salut

    A Fifeshire Prayer
    a shower a shave
    a shit a shag

his father used to
say if shit was
gold you'd have a
wee tyke at yer
erse screamin' faster more

JIMMY AT SIXTEEN
i'm not too strong
on love i just
love to do it

      oh boy a hard-to-find
      piece of freckleton stoneware

one edinburgh publican has
a sign over the
bar that says if
assholes could fly this
would be an airport

     BUDDY HACKETT
     they told him to
     behave as though he
     were an egg he
     lay down on the
     floor they asked him
     what he was doing
     i'm a fried egg

holy cow i said
are you ever huge

sirius listens to dumbledore
even if he doesn't
like what he hears

DIZZY
o john birks you
really were the works

as the french say
may the flames of
islam consume your degenerate
lifestyle you depraved crab-louse

drives like a man
with a paper asshole

a celadon-colored velvet armchair

THELMA'S KITCHEN
black-eyed peas simmer all
day as god intended

we all start plucking
turkeys this next tuesday

tall can of corn

A RICHARD C POEM
the dinah shore dinosaur

bucket of blue smoke

by the way did
you know that massachusetts
is passamaquoddy for asshole

in swim meat 2
the return of humpy
a peter hunter production
here's young jeremy the
classic california blond ditz
so young so dumb
so full of cum
so jeremy intrudes into
a small orgy yelling
better watch out boys
i'ma pig for hole
words for the ages

simon spent most of
the day in the
phone box down there
by the duck pond

had seen that someday
the summer sun would
not throw his shadow

save your bones for
henry jones cause henry
don't eat no meat

APOLLO AND HYACINTHUS
i trust you heeded
your mother's admonition to
wear clean knickers in
case you happened to
meet a god in
the course of your
sultry travels so when
we come to yon
bosky dell i am
likely to rip those
knickers right off you
kid i really am

the rolling stone interview
asked dolly parton if
she was a virgin
in the cheerleader photo
when she was sweet
16 listen here boys
my cherry was so
far up inside me
i used it for
a taillight bless jesus

the irish working class
is uniquely literate in
the western world for
example two englishmen on
a london building site
one says to the
other fucking hell stewart
why are you still
hiring these fucking paddies
after all the bombings
and all i'll tell
you why mate they're
very very intelligent he
calls over paddy paddy
tell my friend the
difference between a joist
and a girder sure
and begorra dead easy
boss joist wrote ulysses
and girder wrote faust

my daughter can spot
a cute boy at
150 yards what she
can't find is a
tomato in the refrigerator

i just had sex
on the coney island
ferris wheel it was
not a dream and
boy am i glad

Das Lied Von Der
Kinderspielplatz
if i give you
a nickel you can
suck my pickel if
you give me a
dime you can suck
it all the time

Stan Getz (1927–1991)
i've never played a
note i didn't mean
and i'd like that
written on my tombstone

it was just yesterday
afternoon wizard whateley said
ygnaiih ygnaiih thflthkhh'ngha yog-sothoth

Lou Donaldson
pickin' coleslaw in arkansas

but by the end
of lunch uncle norman
was enthusing about the
smell of children's armpits

C.S.L.
if you ordered a
trainload of assholes and
all you got was
him you would still
think you got a
lot for your money

OLD 6th-CENTURY-B.C. JOKE
ABOUT AN IONIAN
PHYSIOLOGUE
into the same river
no man steps 2,147
times but who's counting

HOMAGE TO ERSKINE LANE
even then i knew
batman sucked him night
after night in the
tenebrific batcave robin's juicy
little cock all sweaty
and musky after a
hard day's work in
the tireless struggle against
the forces of evil

what's your favorite irish
joke my favorite irish
joke is what's green
and stays out at
night give up the
answer is patio furniture

it was in a
dance hall in leadville
colorado in 1883 that
oscar wilde saw a
sign that seemed to
him the only rational
instance of art criticism
he'd ever beheld it
said please do not
shoot the piano player
he's doing his best

please spell einojujani rautavaara

when the relaxed moment
becomes the right moment
grate 5 cialis tablets
into the scrambled eggs
lock all the doors
close all the curtains
wear a calvinistic jockstrap
send us a report

the stage delicatessen still
deals gently with iowans
who don't know which
is the bagel and
which is the lox

surely the best faux-epitaphe
pour son sepulchre ever
penned is by john
cheever it goes i
never disappointed a hostess
and i never took
it up the butt

tad tomkins was interviewing
the ineffable andy warhol
and the ineffable one
got in first and
asked do you have
a big cock tomkins
thought he'd asked do
you have a big
clock so he said
not especially and glanced
furtively at his wrist

LA GRANDE CUISINE CORRNICHE
soggy ratty tatty oggy

BIG ERMA
i might be too
old to cut the
mustard but i can
still lick the jar

out on the olympic
peninsula in western washington
there are a couple
of nickel towns four
miles apart named sappho
and beaver and about
fifty miles farther south
of that is a
place named humptulips yet
farther south are satsop
and queets without no
doubt aliens have landed
call the white house
dubya knows about them
aliens bein' one himself

GARY CARDEN REPORTS
FROM THE COFFEEHOUSE IN SYLVA
whatzit you readin' carden
jonathan williams izat the
funny feller you must
be thinking of winters
hell yes down to
20 degrees this morning

jeffrey bernard put an
advert in the spectator
veteran alcoholic diabetic amputee
requires sympathy fuck aye
he'll be lucky chuck

as gifts to friends
mencken signed gideon bibles
compliments of the author

never say die says
salman rushdie my next
book will be titled
buddha that fat bastard

A Pot By Yasuhiro Kohara
the elusive wabi sabi

on to the top
of the hill where
the osage oranges grow

the first biblical threesome
shadrach meshach and tobedwego

rude dudes down south
call the female perineum
the taint i.e. taint
pussy taint asshole but
up in civilized new
england the puritan gentlemen
simply call it the
now as in that
fine old song i
wonder who's kissing her
now how very extraordinary

two things don't work
as well after 70
i don't remember what
the second one is

in the wonderful insect
display at the buffalo
science museum is a
sign that ought to
stop you in your
tracks if all the
offspring from one pair
of flies were to
live in four months
191,010,000,000,000,000,000 flies would be
produced covering the earth
47 feet deep wow

size matters sighs matter

the french enjoy westerns
with subtitles i like
the one where the
cowboy pushes through the
swinging doors heists himself
onto a bar stool
the bartender turns around
and says howdy and
the cowboy says enchanté

here's a lovely jewish
joke back in the
old days edward dahlberg
got on a streetcar
in kansas city and
sat behind a distinguished
looking black man wearing
a little yarmulke and
reading a hebrew newspaper
right to left right
to left dahlberg couldn't
resist he tapped his
companion on the shoulder
du bist a yid
the black man turned
around and shrugged heavily
oi veh duss iss
alles vuss felt mir

HOMAGE TO LEE SMITH
one-eyed jesse waldron lives
all by hissef up
in the paw-paw gap

—◦∘◦—

justine poole always says
fuckin is fine as
far as it goes

elvis is alive and
she's beautiful said madonna
after meeting kd lang

B.B. KING
nobody loves me but
my mama and she
may be jivin too

there's a great joke
in thomas adcock's new
detective novel devil's heaven
you know the definition
of an irish homosexual
it's a mick who
prefers women to whiskey

i hear you do
not care greatly for
the fair sex the
fair sex he snapped
back which is that

edmund gosse was so
excited by one of
baron von gloeden's photographs
of a naked sicilian
shepherd boy he took
peeks during robert browning's
funeral service in westminster
abbey and john addington
symonds caught him red-handed

HOMAGE TO VANCE RANDOLPH
the cabin boy the
cabin boy the dirty
little nipper he filled
his ass with broken
glass and circumcised the
skipper bloody masterpiece mate

ira kurlander says the
goddesses adorning the capitals
of bernard maybeck's palace
of fine arts look
like seventy-two lesbians all
busy writing bad checks

CORONATION STREET
and it's me that's
lost me job and
all you want to
think about is a
bit of the rumpy-pumpy

and fred ducketts fits
up the great templates

i borage bring courage

according to peter taylor
a reform club member
three things for proper
gentlemen to remember are
never shoot south of
the thames never follow
whisky with port never
have your wife in
the morning as the
day may have something
much better to offer

G.K. CHESTERTON SENDS
A TELEGRAPH TO HIS WIFE
am in wolverhampton where
ought i to be

HAWKSHEAD, CUMBRIA
visitor is this a
pottery gallery staff no
this is where we
are showing beatrix potter's
pictures visitor turning to
a friend hear that
jack they're showing films

parliament is considering lowering
the age of male
consent to 42 to
cope with the wave
of unbridled dust now
sweeping the british public

Persons in Paradise Gardens
what were they all
but skeletons given a
few years of life

      dear elvis thank you
      for carpeting all the
      ceilings of our hearts

greg norman started birdie
birdie birdie birdie birdie
birdie even the australian
press corps were moved
to vacate the bar

      beating luminous wings in
      the void in vain

      copperhead in the hemerocallis

      hag worm haw moss

mushy peas and pie
a genuine manchester blanket-raiser

cincinnati september 11 1985
after 23 seasons 3,476
games and 13,768 at
bats pete rose finally
got the 4,192nd hit
of his major league
career wednesday night and
passed the greatest batsman
in baseball history ty
cobb writes thomas boswell
in the washington post
the historic hit which
comes 57 years to
the day since cobb's
last at bat was
clean hard and convincing
but credit mickey mantle
for the funniest reaction
to the great event
sayeth the mick hell
if i'da hit that
many singles hell's fire
i'da wore a dress

                    i know a painter
                    in new york city
                    who has slept with
                    forty people who have
                    died of aids incredibly
                    he's still alive painting
                    as vacuously as ever

our distinguished friend the
photographer orcenith lyle bongé
sure hears some mean
jokes when the good
bankers and pharmacists of
old biloxi gather for
refreshment at the yacht
club for instance it's
hard to top this
one for sheer viciousness
you know why black
folks smell different from
white folks give up
the answer is so
blind people can hate
them too that's terrible

R.J. PHONES FROM SAN FRANCISCO
sorry to interrupt dinner
won't keep you just
wanted to tell you
i tested serum negative
and that melanoma thing
they think they got
all of it bye
hope you enjoy dinner

LORD ALFRED DOUGLAS
he was even better
looking than john gray
and even less talented

granted life has always
been lively in the
environs of newbury berkshire
but do you really
think ralph chubb had
sex with twin 16-year-olds
in an abandoned windmill
outside of goldfinch bottom

DAWN SONG IN THE PENNINE DALES
ee wakey wakey wakey
git hands off snakey

THE PASSION OF SAINT PEE-WEE
i like to use
the term manipulating the
genitalia said police lieutenant
bill stookey when interviewed
don't ask me why

martin heidegger german author
and philosopher writings deal
obsessively with term being

what a fine sentence
from tony hillerman's the
ghostway the wing of
the corn beetle affects
the direction of the
wind the way the
sand drifts the way
the light reflects into
the eye of a
man beholding his reality

    the fbi files on
    the late emile de
    antonio included the information
    that when he was
    ten years old he
    told someone he wanted
    to be an eggplant
    when he grew up

doctor william e bradshaw
professor of biology university
of oregon has received
a guggenheim fellowship to
study population dynamics of
british tree-hole mosquitoes dear
god it's about time

THE VENICE BIENNALE
ask to see a
bellini and it's fifty
fifty whether you end
up in front of
a quattrocento masterpiece or
a bar serving bad
champagne and peach juice

jesse helms's high school
principal and band teacher
was ray house and
ray says jesse and
me talked about them
robert mapplethorpe pictures and
what was in there
it's objectionable it's not
for good decent folk
cubism was bad enough
with all them people
riding them bicycles backwards

THE THIRD NICKELSVILLE, VIRGINIA,
SUMMER FESTIVAL
satan said i been
the devil for all
my life but i
never seen hell till
i seen your wife

at 10:15 on the
evening of november 27
at a club called
the cat's cradle in
chapel hill mojo nixon
and the toad lickers
launched themselves into a
song mojo says he
learned from a daughter
of senator jesse helms
a fine christian woman
with knockers big enough
to open heaven's gate
it's called she's got
a louisiana lip-lock on
my love-porkchop see mojo's
becoming much more lyrical

cheeky joan who serves
bar snacks at the
barbon inn whispered rather
loudly to the consternation
of five twits and
confusion of eleven moles
if you've had anything
lately big as these
cumberland sausages love you'll
have been reet lucky
i said to joan
joan you're much too
much for chinese television
aye you really are

mother said can't you
play something christmassy i
said well i just
played you the complete
nutcracker by michael tilson
thomas last year i
tried delius's walk to
the paradise garden and
she said can't you
play something pretty well
it is very hard
to please your mother
what if i tried
leroy anderson sleigh ride
might ring the gong
but then she'd say
don't you have any
strauss waltzes and i'd
say well maybe tomorrow
i need some sleep
we'll start with arnie
schoenberg's gurrelieder and get
that danube really blue

JIMMY ROWLES (1918–1996)
a voice like a
canoe being dragged slowly
across an abandoned road

on the west door
of st. catherine's church
hoarwithy is set forth
a table of kindred
and affinity a man
may not marry his
mother daughter father's mother
mother's mother son's daughter
daughter's daughter sister father's
daughter mother's daughter wife's
mother wife's daughter father's
wife son's wife father's
father's wife mother's father's
wife wife's father's mother
wife's mother's mother wife's
son's daughter wife's daughter's
daughter son's son's wife
daughter's son's wife father's
sister mother's sister brother's
daughter sister's daughter for
a woman it is
the same only different

ah the joys of
rambling the uplands of
britain one day we
were supping ale in
the new inn at
appletreewick in wharfedale appletreewick
by the way of
the esoteric laws of
yorkshire tyke is pronounced
aptrick by the locals
well the new inn
was notorious for the
policies of the old
fart who ran the
place there was no
smoking boots to be
left outside and if
he didn't like your
looks no beer either
just the sort of
divine misanthrope you want
running a public house
anyway we supped timidly
in a corner when
two battle-axes in tweed
skirts and hairy legs
came booming in do
you serve bags of
crisps the publican looked
up slowly from his
deep perusal of volume
two of oswald spengler
and remarked we serve
bags of no kind
absolutely no kind madame

walk 21 is a
beauty westerdale kensgriff and
yarlside but not on
a vile day like
this one so it
made total sense to
repair to the barbon
inn have a few
pints of theakston's best
bitter and be entertained
by some of the
honorable p v taylor's
repertory of bawdy songs
such as the one
that begins i'm tired
of women i'm tired
of whisky and all
of them things but
oh for the joy
of a peach-bottom'd boy
with an arse like
a jelly on springs
please nina give mr
taylor a large glenmorangie
for such savage lyricism
thanks nina cheers peter

a bizarre old thing
cornish torbock hath popped
his clogs he was
the first boy at
eton allowed to attend
chelsea flower show his
ruinous mansion by salvin
in the country southeast
of appleby was splendid
his collection of english
watercolours was biggest and
worst in the country
he was fond of
saying his friends called
him la grande corniche
a grand age 88

dear i hope you
don't think i'm too
old-fashioned but do you
think you could call
me grandmother or grandma
instead of just butt-head

the coroner in east
palo alto who upon
discovering the dead baby
found in a garbage
can was only a
cashew nut said thursday
was a reminder that
everybody makes mistakes everybody

CATWEASEL
he told us he
had a powerful transmitter
and that thursday evenings
were the best time
to get through to
venus said one sedbergh
neighbour but he used
to say a lot
of things indeed so

LEONARD BERNSTEIN (1918–1990)
i like what lenny
told the new york
post maybe people think
of me as just
another pinko faggot a
bleeding heart a do-gooder
but that's what i
am and i'm an
artist too don't forget
lenny we won't forget

PATRICK WHITE
whispers on the radio
that the most familiar
sound in his native
land is the plop
plop of australian bullshit

monika darling how very
nice to see you
this was a lunch
party at beacon house
at langbar overlooking wharfedale
and after lunch monika
the german wife of
a yorkshireman who makes
boilers turned to josephine
our hostess and said
how amusing to meet
civilized americans the remark
of the season i
long to have had
the wit to reply
do you know that
remark by one of
the mitford girls the
thing i liked most
about hitler was his
hands he'd lovely hands

rothko i remember the
time one couple looked
at red brown and
black she was in
a rapture she was
ecstatic and he said
hey it looks like
our old tv set
i kind of sympathized
with the man because
at the time i
had an old tv
set myself no question
rothko makes you think
says alec sologob a
guard at moma bastard's
on duty 2,000 hours
year in year out

A BASIL BUNTING MEMORIAL BUMPER-STICKER

FUCK ME I'M FIREPROOF

MISTER FRANCIS BACON VISITS HIS RETROSPECTIVE AT THE HIRSHHORN MUSEUM IN WASHINGTON

a respectable person from
winston-salem north carolina suddenly
pauses midway in the
exhibition lest there be
the smoking remains of
a terrible three-car crash
in the next room
guard she asks do
people like these paintings
lady if you think
these are bad you
shudda seen him he
was here last week

            no rat can relax

in italy one is
only allowed eleven words
per postcard so ciao
i missed by one

            so life goes on
            very much like a
            piece by morty feldman

POEM BEGINNING WITH FIVE WORDS BY
GERARD MANLEY HOPKINS

glory be to god
for jesse helms jesse
hates fags jesse hates
niggers jesse hates modern
art now that one
thinks about it jesse's
just like most people
in north carolina and
everywhere else what jesse
likes is beauty and
beauty's what bites you
on the butt and
don't leave a hickey
on monday morning we
must be kind to
jesse helms you must
brake for senior republican
senators from north carolina
he has the law
on his sidewinder snake
in the grass that
he is whether he
will brake for us
poets and artsnakes is
another matter thank you
jesus thanks a bunch

—⊙—

and remember to die

II. MAHLER

A NOTE FOR THE FIRST EDITION (Marlborough Portfolio, 1965)

My time has not yet come, but your time is always ready.
— Mahler

It would seem, finally, that *response* is the most necessary function for us — as men and as artists. I find it put exactly by Robert Duncan's lines from the poem "The Law I Love Is Major Mover":

Responsibility is to keep
the ability to respond.

Since I first heard a performance of Gustav Mahler's *Symphony No. 1, in D Major* by the Philadelphia Orchestra under Eugene Ormandy on November 8, 1949, in Carnegie Hall, New York, I have been more responsive to his music than to any other. In other words, for some fifteen years now. And so it seems fitting, in May 1964, when the Yellow-Billed Cuckoo has returned to these mountains and intimately evokes the First Symphony, to practice these exercises in spontaneous composition to the movements of all the Mahler symphonies. I am interested in gauging my response in compositions of language to the sounds of the music, not in imitating the sounds, which would be futile and silly. My desire to make this homage to Mahler is well expressed by the critic Paul Stefan in his book, *Gustav Mahler: A Study of His Personality and Work* (G. Schirmer, New York, 1913). Stefan is quoting Schopenhauer as his principal witness: "Our age...sees in this life (the sluggish blood of the Too-Many never yet succeeded in attaining to *life*) only sin and lamentation, hurry and restlessness. At best it seeks hastily and superficially to conform itself to it, oftenest in the end condemning it as superficial. And therefore our 'men of culture,' those who 'acknowledge' our time, 'make an end as quickly as possible of everything, works of art, beautiful natural objects, and the really valuable view of life in all its scenes.'"

48

In his very useful insights, Stefan says at another point: "In general, the hearer who interprets rather than listens likes nothing better than to investigate what the composer 'meant' by his works. Of course, he meant nothing whatever. But by means of a symbol, an image, one may better understand his works. Beethoven's headings and instructions and Schumann's titles are intended to be thus understood, and in this sense Mahler's symphonies can here and there be described in words; often the words of the vocal movements themselves invite it." He mentions for instance the programme that Mahler attached to early performances of the First Symphony in Hamburg and Weimar: "Part I. The Days of Youth. Youth, flowers and thorns. (1) Spring without end. The introduction represents the awakening of nature at early dawn. (Nota: in Hamburg it was called 'Winter Sleep.') (2) A Chapter of Flowers (Andante). (3) Full Sail (Scherzo)," and so on. He then quotes the young Bruno Walter: "Let us be prudent enough to free these titles from an exact meaning, and remember in the kingdom of beauty nothing is to be found except *Gestaltung, Umgestaltung, des ewigen Sinnes ewige Unterhaltung.* (Formation, Transformation, the Eternal Mind's Eternal Recreation.)... We must not think of that 'which the flowers of the meadow tell,' but of everything that touches our hearts with gentlest beauty and tenderest charm."

So, then, these responses to the music. They were written *only* during the duration of each movement, lest the composing get too elaborated. The titles are simply the musical markings of the movements, in my amateur translations. I have used earphones to listen to the recordings in my collection, which serve to blot out extraneous background noise and enhance the concentration. Another useful exercise might be to draw with the eyes shut, using only the motor faculty while listening with closest attention. This is a technique we employed at Moholy-Nagy's Institute of Design in Chicago to "liberate" response.

Finally, while the poems are spontaneous and reworked once or twice at the most (during a second performance of a movement), the background for writing them is not random. I am calling upon fifteen years of performances, recordings, and readings. Of the First Symphony, I am fortunate to have heard it in person by Ormandy, Walter, Kubelik, Barbirolli, and Mitropoulos; and on records also by Kletzki, Leinsdorf, Boult, Horenstein, Scherchen, and Steinberg. The books I have are by Alma Mahler, Dika Newlin, Schoenberg, Krenek, Guido Adler, Paul Stefan, Richard Specht, and Bruno Walter. I regret that I cannot read the collection of Mahler's own letters (1879–1911), not available yet (I think) in English. My other information is everything else I know and am moved by. To end with Paul Stefan: "The music, dewy fresh, strikes the goggles from the nose of the peering critic."

Jonathan Williams
Highlands, North Carolina
May–June 1964

A NOTE FOR THE SECOND EDITION (Cape Golliard, 1969)

R.B. Kitaj, the old Chagrin Falls Flash and Tracer of Lost Persons, picked up the poems and ran with them. Quoting his "Mahler: A Celebration and a Crutch" (in the exhibition catalogue of the Marlborough-Gerson Gallery, New York, February, 1965): "Jonathan Williams has written 40 poems responding to Mahler's symphonies and I have begun (Fall 1964) to make a run of prints using the music, the poems, the Mahler literature and times and a good deal else as a compound crutch upon which to hang much that cannot be made to splice easily with Mahler. In this light Mahler's own ambiguous, lifelong attitude towards 'The vexed problem of programme music' is worth noting and he reminds us that 'The creative urge for a musical organism certainly springs from an experience of its author, i.e., from a fact, after all, which should be positive enough to be expressible in words,' and also that 'My music arrives at a programme as its last clarification, whereas in the case of Richard Strauss the programme already exists as a given task...'

"Thanks are due to H.R. Fischer for his encouragement of the work at hand which will often spring from music which he knows in ways I never will and to Chris Prater, who is printing the work...much of the essence of the thing is in his hands. We hope to bring out the prints one day in an edition of 50 on various papers with the Williams sequence in the place of honour..."

Marlborough Fine Art Limited, London, did in fact publish the suite of screen prints (15 in number) together with a book of the original 40 poems. Printed by Tillotsons; designed by Gordon House; 30 copies in commerce, numbered and signed by the poet; issued in the summer of 1967.

For the present edition by *Cape Goliard Press Limited,* Kitaj has kindly prepared special covers, in lieu of the screen prints which would cost you about 400 guineas. The sinister portrait of the poet on the title page is from Kitaj's painting, *Aureolin* (1964), of Col. J. Williams (Musical Director of the Macon County North Carolina Meshuga Sound Society).

Minor adjustments, clarifications, and (hopefully) improvements have been made on the poems of symphonies 1 through 9. The Tenth Symphony is new. When I wrote the others in the spring of 1964 I did not have available a recording of Deryck Cooke's "performing version" of the symphony with the five movements complete. Eugene Ormandy's performance of this score on Columbia is a very fine one, and he and Mr. Cooke, particularly, deserve our thanks. The one movement, the Adagio, I knew from the Tenth is now rewritten and joined by the rest of the work. I would like to put on the earphones again in about ten years and see what Mahler has to tell me. The message appears to be coming in louder and clearer, what with this Christmas's package of nine symphonies and *Das Lied* by Bernstein; and the likelihood of similar collections from DGG and Victor within another year or two. I hope not to be put off by these astonishing populist developments and chased back into the arcanum of the 90-year-old gent who wrote the *Universe Symphony,* or the *Turangalila* of Messiaen, or Goldmark, or Schrecker, or Medtner, or Kurt Atterburg, who finished the Unfinished Symphony. I think not. As a matter of fact I am conducting an investigation into the number of cuckoos in the First Symphony of Mahler—mimetic or purely musical intervals. Dr. Herbert Brün is my accomplice, and the results will show when I next sit down to write my findings, perhaps in March 1979 in the West Riding of Yorkshire.

Jonathan Williams
Aspen Institute for Humanistic Studies
Aspen, Colorado 81611
December 8, 1967

SYMPHONY No. 1, IN D MAJOR

*...to write a symphony means, to me, to
construct a world with all the tools of
the available technique. The ever-new and
changing content determines its own form.*
—Mahler, 1895

I. *Slowly–dragging, like a sound of nature*

Moravian plains...dawn...horns and bassoons down below
dawn...

o hello, cuckoos,
hello, bluebells and bugles
in a spring rain

Orpheus strings the wind with the mind's
night soil and sewage

kling! kling!

o yes, Linnaeus,
"the marsh marigold blows when the cuckoo sings!"

and the sunshine
sings

and the sunshine sings
all things

open

II. *Strongly agitated, but not too fast*

it's doubtful whether
rustic Austrian bees,
as described by Professor von Frisch,
dance round
sunny boxwoods so
stately, so ceremoniously as
this

but, brown thrashers in dirt, chirping 3/4 time—
yes

III. *Solemn and measured, without dragging*

two blue eyes
too blew ayes
to loose ice...

        merrily down the
        merrily verily merrily verily
        down the stream

        where *la vida*
        es sueño is

        a dream
        down the stream
        under the *linden*
        baum

ice, yes, eyes
streamed

IV. *Stormily agitated*

the things seen, the
intervals, and the noises
are nature's, Dr.
Williams:

"Measure serves for us as the key:
we can measure between objects;
therefore we know that they
exist."

lichens on aspens
seen in green
lightning

the crack of perception isn't too quick,
the cuckoo's call is tuned by
andrenal glands,
clouds linked to the world
by lightning and tuning—it cracks the
stones and melts the heart

the cuckoo takes heart, eye-bright
in blue air, lightning

hits it

SYMPHONY No. 2, IN C MINOR

What is the answer?
What was the question?
— Gertrude Stein (last words)

I. *"Pompes Funèbres": briskly, majestically, with complete*
gravity & solemnity of expression

"why live, why
suffer?

because of a
great joke, an
absurd joke?

we ask these old
questions, to

continue to live
to continue
dying..."

an empyrean hand
touching the
stem of
a great gold sunflower

in absolute
silence

a farina of seeds filling
the sky

in absolute
silence

II. *Moderately slow: "Schubertian"*

sun
on
rain
clouds

summer sun
on
ploughed
clods

paeans of
loud
sunshine

III. *"St. Anthony of Padua's Sermon to the Fishes":*
   in a quiet, flowing motion

> Padua's Anthony's
> ichthyo-euphony—
> yeah! yeah! yeah!
>
> sermon's over
> fish same as ever—
> blah! blah! blah!
>
> stupidity today!
> moribundity tomorrow!
> rah! rah! rah!

IV. *"Primeval Light": very solemn, but simple*

"in an artist
it must come from
a sense of totality; the whole;
and humanity as a whole.
How can a man be satisfied
when he sees another man
lacking ——"

I am from God, and
must to God return

While we slept these kept with us:
the grosbeak's breast in the early sun,
the wood thrush's notes, ants
in the leaves,
mallows in the wind and
dogwoods opening

the world of the little hears little Mahler,
but while we slept
these kept with us

v. *Scherzo tempo: all stops out*

The Lord of Orchards
selects his fruits
in the Firmament's
breast.

"Hogs live in the present;
Poets live in the past,"
said Palmer. Orchards are
where the air
is blessed.

SYMPHONY No. 3, IN D MINOR

Thousands lavishing, thousands starving;
intrigues, wars, flatteries, envyings,
hypocrisies, lying vanities, hollow amusements,
exhaustion, dissipation, death—and giddiness
and laughter, from the first scene to the last.

—Samuel Palmer, 1858

I. *Pan Awakes: Summer Marches In*

Pan's
spring rain
"drives his victims
out to the animals
with whom they become
as one"—

pain and paeans,
hung in the mouth,

to be sung

II. *What the Flowers in the Meadow Tell Me*

June 6, 1857, Thoreau in his *Journal:*

A year is made up of a certain series
and number of sensations and thoughts
which have their language in nature...

Now I am ice, now
I am sorrel.

Or, Clare, 1840, Epping Forest:

I found the poems in the fields
And only wrote them down

and

The book I love is everywhere
And not in idle words

John, *claritas* tells us the words are *not* idle,
the syllables are able
to turn plantains into quatrains,
tune *raceme* to *cyme, panicle* and *umbel* to
form corollas in light clusters of tones...

Sam Palmer hit it:
"Milton, by one epithet
draws an oak of the largest girth I ever saw,
'Pine and *monumental* oak':
I have just been trying to draw a large one in
Lullingstone; but the poet's tree is huger than
any in the park."

Muse in a meadow, compose in
a mind!

III. *What the Animals in the Forest Tell Me*

Harris's Sparrow —

103 species seen
by the Georgia Ornithological Society
in Rabun Gap,

including Harris's Sparrow, with its
black crown, face, and bib encircling
a pink bill

It was, I think, the third sighting
in Georgia, and I should have been there
instead of reading Clare, listening to
catbirds and worrying about
Turdus migratorius that flew
directly into the Volkswagen and
bounced into a ditch

Friend Robin, I cannot figure it, if I'd
been going 40 you might be
whistling in some grass.

10 tepid people got 10 stale letters
one day earlier,
I cannot be happy
about that.

iv. *What the Night Tells Me*

the dark drones on
in the southern wheat fields
and the hop flowers
open before the sun's
beckoning

the end
is ripeness, the wind
rises,
and the dawn says
yes

YES! it says
"yes"

v. *What the Morning Bells Tell Me*

Sounds, and sweet aires
that give delight
and hurt not—

that, let
Shakespeare's
delectation
bear us

VI. *What Love Tells Me*

Anton Bruckner counts the 877th leaf
on a linden tree in the countryside near Wien
and prays:

Dear God, Sweet Jesus,
Save Us, Save Us…

the Light in the Grass,
the Wind on the Hill,

are in my head,
the world cannot be heard

Leaves obliterate
my heart,

we touch each other
far apart…

Let us count
into
the Darkness

SYMPHONY No. 4, IN G MAJOR

...inter urinas et faeces nascimur.
— Saint Augustine

1. *Serene — wary, not hurried*

"Happinesses have wings and wheels;
    miseries are leaden legged,
    and their whole employment is to clip
    the wings and take off the wheels
    of our chariots.
    We determine, therefore, to be happy
    and do all that we can, tho' not
    all that we would,"

said William Blake in Felpham, Sussex

And so there are
    mysterious chariots chanting
    charivaris and planting
    haricots verts
    in the air
    over Thomas Hariot's Cheviot
    potato patch

Everything should be
as simple as
it is,
but *not*
simpler,
agreed Professor
Einstein, a stone's throw
away in Chariot

Eight

11. *In a comfortable motion*

"like a fiend in a cloud,"
Death calls the tune,
plays out of tune and arrives
in a cloud

heard only by the catbird,
who sits in Death's June sunshine
and sings the tune again

and again

and simply continues singing:

black eye/blue sky!
black eye/blue sky!

III. *Restful*

"I live in a hole here,
but God has a beautiful mansion for me elsewhere."

O grow
a Mountain in Fountain
Court

Sundown over
London

Kate Blake
in black

IV. *Very comfortably*

Saint Peter looks on in Heaven,
6 o'clock, Sunday, the 12th of August 1827:

"Lest you should not have heard
of the Death of Mr. Blake
I have written this to inform you...

—Just before he died His Countenance became fair—
His eyes Brighten'd and He burst out in Singing
of the things he Saw in Heaven. In truth He Died
like a Saint as a Person who was standing by Him
Observed..."

No music on earth
is there
that might ever compare
with ours

SYMPHONY No. 5, IN C SHARP MINOR

How blessed, how blessed a tailor to be!
Oh that I had been born a commercial traveller
and engaged as baritone at the Opera! Oh that
I might give my Symphony its first performance
fifty years after my death!
  —Mahler, 1904

I. *Funeral March*

Mahler, from his studio on the eleventh floor of the
Hotel Majestic, New York City, hears the cortege of a
fireman moving up Central Park West:

one roll of the drum

one road where the wind storms, where
Cherubim sing birds' songs
with human faces and hold the world
in human hands and
drift on the gold road
where black wheels smash
all

one roll of the drum

II. *Stormily agitated*

to be a block of flowers
in a wood

to be mindlessly in flower
past understanding

to be shone on
endlessly

to be *there,* there
and blessed

III. *Scherzo*

one two three
one two three

little birds waltz to and fro
in the piano

at Maiernigg on the
Wörthersee

and up the tree:
cacophony

one two three

IV. *Adagietto*

one feels
one clematis petal
fell

its circle
is all

glimmer on this pale
river

v. *Rondo-Finale*

Schoenberg: "I should
even have liked to observe
how Mahler
knotted his tie,

and should have found that
more interesting and instructive
than learning how
one of our musical bigwigs composes
on a 'sacred subject.'

...An apostle
who does not glow
preaches heresy."

his tie was knotted
with éclat
on
the dead run!

SYMPHONY No. 6, IN A MINOR

The life and knowledge of God may doubtless
be described as love playing with itself;
but this idea sinks into triviality, if the
seriousness, the pain, the patience and the
labor of the Negative are omitted.
—Hegel

I. *Brisk, with energy, but not too much*

O Alma, Almschili, Almaschel, Almschi, Almscherl —

the dream
does not know
the word
"no"

Alma Mahler

O Alma! Mater! O Cybele!
Jubilate!

II. *Moderately slow*

"When we're alone for a time we achieve
a unity with ourselves and nature…

we become positive
(instead of stuck in negation)
and finally productive

the commonplace takes us farther and farther
from ourselves
but we are brought back to ourselves
by solitude,
and from ourselves to God
is only a step.

Yes, I am lost to the world
with which I used to waste much time.

I live alone in my heaven,
in my love, in my song."

the cowbells
on the hills

are far
below

III. *Scherzo*

one potato two potato
three potato four

so, off the floor
out the door

to grandfather's
flowers
by the lake-
shore

little girl, that man
is Frankenstein, not your
grandfather

one potato two potato
three potato four,

Mister?

IV. *Finale*

It is the *hero*
on whom fall
three blows of fate,

the last of which
fells him
as a tree is
felled.

"He was a tree
in full leaf
and flower."

SYMPHONY No. 7, IN B MINOR

The poet, no less than the scientist,
works on the assumption that inert and
live things and relations hold enough
interest to keep him alive as part of nature.
—Louis Zukofsky

I. *Adagio*

dark green radiance
beast snarl
yellow shadow

lucidity, touch,
blood, pulse

—⟡—

moon black empyrean fire,
awe,
stone cascade

body, eye, birth,
laugh

II. *Night Music, moderately fast*

the halcyon sun
opens
and captures
night's raging epiphanies

hands love
in a cool wood

—⟳—

poems and paeans
move time
in celebrations

the blue bird
dreams
of hot, coiling play

III. *Like a shadow*

hair
ear

globe
roar

flesh
flash

white
song

spectrum

life
mystery

———❦———

mouth
smile

pleasure
dance

wind
tracery

energy
yield

pool

shining
image

IV. *Night Music, slowly, lovingly*

melodies whir,
muscles glory,

the locale lights,
red embraces,

and ecology
mixes April

———∞———

tones breathe,
touch charges,

and justice circuits:

once-blooming leaves water October earth

v. *Rondo-Finale*

Blake's Mission:

a Flowering Heart,
Delight in the Lungs,

Calm Trance,

a gold cloud
at gloaming

—☙—

Mahler's Vision:

Eternal Atonement,
Music's Exuberance,

Air & Waterfalls

Come, Death-Spirit!

NOTE

Following the lead of Louis Zukofsky's inscription on the viability of the relationships for the poet between "inert and live things," I have made the poems of "Symphony No. 7, in B Minor" through the use of a "Hallucinatory Deck." This is a personal, alchemical deck of 55 white cards on which are written 110 words — the private and most meaningful words of my poetic vocabulary. One then plays with the deck in various ways. In this case, I dealt out 11 cards for each of the five movements of the symphony. In the first movement they are combined but left as simple nouns, verbs, and adjectives. In the second movement, particles have been added and a simple connecting syntax. In the third movement the deal is left as it fell from the deck — 11 cards having 22 words. In the fourth movement, nouns are made to act with verbs. The fifth movement yields a very extraordinary constellation and is the most hallucinatory of the five deals. Around the words *Blake* and *Mahler* the dealer was given a chain of precise meanings which more than justified the use of the deck in the experiment... My knowledge of the deck derives from the poet Michael McClure, who credits the Los Angeles painter George Herms with its invention.

JW

SYMPHONY No. 8, IN E-FLAT MINOR

Nature swells from herring to leviathan,
from the hodmandod to the elephant, so,
divine Art piles mountains on her hills,
and continents upon those mountains.
— Samuel Palmer, 1828

I. *Hymn: "Veni, Creator Spiritus!"*

Since — since — since Brahms,
nothing has been written equal it,
gasped an eccentric American.

Spitting on the floor
does not help you to be Beethoven,
snapped Mahler.

II. *Closing Scene from Goethe's* Faust

all that is transitory
is but an image

a world presented
and fashioned step-by-step —

it will be *actual,*
there will be no paraphrase,
no similitudes and images...

what *actual* need is there of notes?
"I can only say it once more by means of an image":

hemerocallis is
a Goddess's dark orange chalice,
in the blue beyond
the blessed clouds

God (Gustav Mahler) looked
and saw that it was good.

Eros is Creator
of the World.

SYMPHONY No. 9, IN D

To live is to defend a form.
—Anton Webern

I. *Moderately slow*

what will you do, God,
when I am dead?

not quote
Rilke

II. *In the time of an easy Austrian Landler*

We'll go to Egypt and see nothing but blue sky,
we'll walk across water on my matted streptococci—

that will be the day
to be happy

systole, diastole, dance
the holy dance!

III. *Rondo: Burleske*

what's red, bleeds —
and runs in circles?

the miracle
of the art of
the human
heart

in a sweat

IV. *Adagio*

Grinzing cemetery, outside Wien, May 19, 1911:

the sun shone on
on one alone

"*Bless* **re**laxes"

SYMPHONY No. 10, IN F SHARP MINOR

Grace is courage to try to put the world
in order through love.

   —Hildegard Jone

I.

Yea, Lord!
cowbells, cold streams, warm hills, animals
die, we

die... *"ewig, ewig"... Das Lied*
               Von Der Erde

        red red red *Der*
        Erde

Anton Webern's last words were
es ist aus

Hans Moldenhauer's
book on the death
tells us about Raymond N. Bell,
American Army cook,
who fired three shots the night of September 15, 1945,
and killed Webern:

Mount Olive, North Carolina
April 7, 1960

"*...My husband's middle name was Norwood. Date of birth was August 16, 1914. We have one son who will be 21 in June. My husband's occupation was a chef in restaurants. He died from alcoholism (September 3, 1955).*

I know very little about the accident. When he came home from the war he told me he killed a man in the line of duty. I know he worried greatly over it. Everytime he became intoxicated, he would say, 'I wish I hadn't killed that man.' I truly think it helped to bring on his sickness. He was a very kind man who loved everyone. These are the results of war. So many suffer. I do not know any of the details..."

Sincerely,

(Mrs.) Helen S. Bell

> *es ist aus,*
> that's all she wrote,
> buddy...

II. *Scherzo One*

come,
o mod grass-hoppers,
clad in clod-hoppers

the measure is
MEADOW
MEADOW
MEADOW
MEADOW

four,
square

meadows,
with pastures getting the measure of rivers

the measure is
FLOW-
ER
FLOW-
ER
FLOW-
ER
FLOW-
ER

a case of
four
roses,

o cloud-hoppers, clad
in wine-dark sequins —

where it ends with beer gardens
tap dancing, and prancing
small hills dancing
in dance halls

the measure is
MOUNTAIN MOUNTAIN MOUNTAIN MOUNTAIN
MOUNTAIN

"what treads within us
on that red road?"

"next moment
when I leave this room
I shall be just as silly
as all the rest"

III. *Purgatorio*

"The Libido is a
Dolomite;
an Eagle is an Emblem
of Desire"

Alt-Schluderbach
bei Toblach:

in the Composing-Hut,
in the composing heat

something
"frightfully dark"
come in
the open
window

something "frightfully dark":

talons and pinions!

and a crow come
from under
a sofa!

suffocation:

ANGINA!
AQUILA!

"all against all"

a heart made
of red meat

a raven in
the skin

in the hut
in the art

birds
twittering

dead
birds

in
1910

IV. *Scherzo Two*

<blockquote>
"if your taste has been
purified in Berlin,
be prepared
to have it ruined"
</blockquote>

Dear
Pussy Gaylord,
"Possom Galore,"

Mr. Kitty,
poised

in the Showy
Daisy-Flea-Bane

(how sane, how
sanguine it all sounds)

to pounce on
chipmunks
under the porch

Eli, Eli,
lama
sabachthani!

"one often feels one
has got into a pub
or a sty"

the hills
around us
narrow their
yellow eyes
around us;
their claws
click into place
around us

it is a
sunny, bloody,

summer
morning

v. *Finale (Enlargement on Lines by Joel Oppenheimer and Charles Olson)*

against violets —
no defence!

again!
again!

who ran with summer, with
tansy

whose heart
became quiet

in the frost
of the last

chrys-
anthemum

III. APPLE-PIE ORDER

CLERIHEWS

The *clerihew* was invented in 1890 by Edmund Clerihew Bentley, who was a schoolboy of sixteen at St. Paul's in London when the divine numen of Orpheus struck him. His best one seems to me:

> *The digestion of Milton*
> *Was unequal to Stilton.*
>
> *He was only feeling so-so*
> *When he wrote Il Penseroso.*

He never got any better than that, and few people have ever managed to equal him, though such as Auden, John Sparrow, Constant Lambert, James Elroy Flecker, Maurice Hare, and Gavin Ewart have tried. I can recall one sublime effort:

> *How odd*
> *of God*
>
> *to choose*
> *the Jews.*

This was written by the now-obscured World War One poet William Norman Ewer (1885–1976). It makes me quote the equally sublime rebuttal by Leo Rosten, (as someone says,) the Yiddishist:

> *Not odd*
> *of God.*
>
> *Goyim*
> *annoy'im!*

E.C. Bentley went on to Oxford, was a lifelong friend of G.K. Chesterton, wrote editorials for *The Daily Telegraph* for more than twenty years, and is remembered as the author of the detective novel *Trent's Last Case.*

Frances Stillman's *The Poet's Manual and Rhyming Dictionary* (1965) says this: "The clerihew is a humorous pseudo-biographical quatrain, rhymed as two couplets, with lines of uneven length, and often contains or implies a moral reflection of some kind. The name of the individual who is the subject of the quatrain usually supplies the first line."

Never read James Dickey
when the weather's hot and icky.

The time for dickey-dunkin
's when de frost is on de punkin.

Babe Ruth
in all truth

weren't borned like you an' me —
he come down out of a tree.

Hesiod
is seldom read.

His *Works and Days*
irks most guys.

Stevie Smith
invited Death

to live with her
and eat verdure.

Mombi the Witch
had an itch

to be a Girl Goddess
like Robert Duncan in his Eleusinian, pearl headdress.

Ezra Loomis Pound
bought a lb

of Idaho potatoes
(the Hailey Comet always ate those).

Why did Professor J.R.R. Tolkien
never really come clean

about the scientologists in cupboards
in the House of L. Ron Hubbard?

Li Tai Po
please telepho-

ne Mnemosyne,
straight away!

David Hockney
met a most *ravissant* Cockney

with, *mirabile dictu,*
no cock to hang onto!

Hank D. Thoreau
too seldom used eau

de cologne,
and was asked to live at Walden on his own.

Sir Edward Elgar
was never vulgar,

though why — in mixed company — he made jokes about smegma
was certainly an enigma.

Percy Grainger
was no stranger

to stinging whips
and Mother's lips.

Puccini
is arguably better than zucchini.

But a pound of spinach
could write a better symphony than Zdeněk Fibich.

Ross Lee Finney
left North Dakota because he wasn't getting any

Tartini, dodecaphony,
or even weenie.

They say Herman "The Hunk" Melville was given to itches
to get into Mr. Nathaniel Hawthorne's britches.

But, there is no evidence that Queequeg
ever went whole hog.

John Blow
was below

par when he wrote "Cloe Found Amintas Lying
On a Pile of Swedes Near Dorking."

Mr. Charles Edward Ives
vies

with Spike Jones, John Philip Sousa, and Scott Joplin
for being The Number One All-American.

Ralph Vaughan Williams
munches now on trilliums…

having contrived in earthly clay just how
to write sweet music very like a cow.

John Cage
bestrode his age.

"FUCK ZEN!"
chimes in the octogenarian Huck Finn.

Charles Tomlinson Griffes
was said to have the stiffest

dork
in refined musical circles in all of Elmira, New York.

Alma Mahler
could really holler!

On those odd, ur-Freudian occasions when she took it up the butt,
she often hit fortissimo high-C and commenced doing the "Danube Strut."

Leoš Janáček
in photographs looks a bloody blank Czech.

His music, as it unfurls,
appeals mostly to squirrels.

Franz Liszt
even played the piano when he pissed.

It was odd to see his piano stool dripping
during performances of *Années de Pèlerinage* that were absolutely gripping!

THE BARON

Both bodacious & humongous
was large Charles Mingus.

On both mouth & bass
—he played his ass!

Thomas Wolfe
wolfed

herds
of words.

Said Morgan Foster
over some oysters:

"Only Connect-
icut!"

NEAR WHINNY HAW

Climbing Firbank Fell,
Ronald Firbank fell

about laughing
at two heifers fucking.

SUNT LACRIMAE RERUM

The truth is William Blake
is hard to take

for those of us with earthy ears
and eyes the size of tiny deer's.

LES MATINS DANS LA RUE DE FLEURUS, NO. 27

Gertrude Stein
arose at nine

and arose and arose
and arose.

Clara Hughes, the author of these clerihews,
wrote them strictly to chase the blues.

"Gee, I think they're neat,"
said her illiterate girlfriend, Pete.

LIMERICKS

There was an old sod named GOD
by vast numbers of very odd
people impressed by steeples
full of spiritual peepholes
to look out all over the crud.

O BLASYNGE STERRE!

There was an old comet named Halley
with a tail shaped like a shillelagh.
When it came into orbit
the earthlings mistook it
for an haute-cuisine carrot in aioli.

JOHN SELL COTMAN

Assessing the angle of Ingleborough
caused Cotman to dangle his single bore
in a glish bit of clay,
mixcd with Paine's grey,
he kept in a monochrome shingle burrow.

There once was a slut named Salome
who liked guys with *molto* salami!
She'd cut off the head
of anything red
that was soft, or seemed dead, or too smarmy.

There was an old Fauré named Gabe
who kept a dead whore in his cave.
"Wrong line, you fool,
Gabe saves his tool
for seraphs and boys who don't shave."

A number I met in Toronto
spoke extremely bad Esperanto.
For fuckin' and suckin'
he preferred being stuck in
a threesome involving his right toe.

There once was a poet named Sappho
who wrote deathless words on her dildo.
It wasn't just twat
that got her all hot—
it's a shame she couldn't play banjo.

There was an old knitter of Dent
whose sock was so long that it went
quite funny in the middle
and often filled with piddle
and was of no use for the rent.

A lady from Fuquay-Varina
had a very outré vagina.
It liked to play tricks
on guys with thick pricks
by grinding their balls to farina.

The composer named Charles Edward Ives
wrote stuff that gave people hives.
Though "Booth Led Boldly..."
the Republic got moldy,
and in Danbury little still thrives.

A Quaker lass down at Brigflatts
was done by five fun-loving cats.
But along came George Fox
and cut off their cocks
and bought her some feathery hats.

A nelly young novice from Crewe
said, "Why should I do it with you?
The Vicar is slicker — and quicker —
and very much thicker,
and three inches longer than you!"

There was a composer from Quimper
who taught his asshole to whimper,
and then to sing scales
that cut right through gales
and caused all his critics to simper.

A salacious old farmer from Oughtershaw
had his willie reupholstered in straw;
and he tickled the hearts
and diverse private parts
of ladies from S(cunt)horpe to (Clit)heroe.

ACROSTICALS

A TUNED-ROW OF ADJECTIVES & A PSALMODIC TOAST
for Stefan Wolpe at 68

S: SALAMANDRINE, meaning able to survive in fire...

T: TERRESTRIOUS, having the nature of earth; earthy...

E: ETHEREOUS, composed of the upper element of the universe

F: FLUXIVE, i.e., variable; apt to flow...

A: AKASHIC (Sanskrit), of the subtle matter imagination
      is made from —

N: Nothing for this heavy elemental load
      but Apollo's very own nepenthes
      delivered daily to your door...

W: We of the West Riding of Yorkshire/Buncombe County

O: O-Lieber-Komposer-Feller Gesellschaft

L: Loudly

P: Proclaim

E: Each generation shall praise thy works to another!

from LETTERS FROM LEXINGTON
(Acrostical Portrait #6)

Greens, corn bread & buttermilk!

Un griot des yeux, a summoner of spirits!

You know damned well Stephen Foster was a Pennsylvanian!

Depthless still life on the Shaker Apple Sauce label!

Aye God, a very Oread!

Von Herzen kommen!

"Entropy is never random: it is always one negative tetrahedron!"

"Never trust a man with a little prick!"

Pancho Villa's Revolutionary hotdogs with Emiliano Zapata chili!

One appreciates "nipscop tickfaw moodus!"

Rejoice in the rhododendrons and wild dogwoods!

To keep afloat the Ark of Culture in these dark and tacky times!

THE TERRIBLE KNITTERS OF DENT
FABRICATE A NATALITIAL FRAGMENT
FOR THE ACROSTICAL MISTER BUNTING
ON HIS 70th BIRTHDAY, BY THE TYNE,
MARCH 1, 1970

Building a poem: The first requirement is to have good quoins.
A line and a rule would guide a fool, a saying runs.
Set off right or you can't finish a roof—or a poem or a life.
In order to addle a living, set off in the dark for the far fells,
Loaf and some onions for food, built two roods a day.

Bewick was one; you, another—able to wall the gap in the tradition,
Unerring in the words to use for walling poems—
Not difficult for a man with good hands and a straight eye.
The wisdom of keeping a headstone in the parlour to carve in winter
Is obvious, like swallowing lots of tea when there is any.
Note: "The work should be simple," say the Poem-Masons of Swaledale.
Good poems, like good walls, stand 60 to 100 years and never budge.

ROCOCO DEFINITIONS FOR MODESTO (CALIFORNIA)'S ONLY AMBULATORY 60-YEAR-OLD ALECTRYOMANCER
(Acrostical Portrait #5)

J stands for *Jehu,*
who strews Bay Area eros
as he goes

A stands for *Alveary,*
the hive where the words hum;
the hollow of the outer ear
where song waxes and wax sings

M stands for *Modesto,*
as in Addison's line:
"An excess of Modesto
obstructs the Tongue."

E stands for *Enneacontahedral,*
having ninety faces,
though we see
only his one
in these preempyrean days,

above a pair of dancing boots
the color of larks' spurs
on the edge
of the desert

S stands for *Simurgh,*
the monstrous bird
of Persian legend,

imagined as rational
and of great age...

ok for the rare bird
of the San Joaquin
to be old,
but not *rational*

B stands for *Bed,*
      as in the film *The Bed:*
      the Bedstead
      under the Bodhi Tree
      was so full of bodies
      sparks lit the sky

R stands for *Rallentando,*
      because it has
      an ent
      in it
      (for slowly being entheate
      in a sacred wood)

O stands for *Ockfen* —
      Ja, a case of Ockfener Bockstein
      to toast tonight's occasion!

      170 years ago to the day
      Coleridge in the Lake District
      looked out his window at 7:15...

      he was impressed
      by an enormous cloud
      in the shape of an egg,

      so give Sam a drink, too

U stands for *Uropygial,*
    situated on
    or belonging to the rump
    in birds, what
    a word!

G stands for *Gizzard,*
    the name of the izzard
    James used to walk
    along Stinson Beach
    on days "gray as chamois"

H stands for *Humbuggery,*
    I mean:
    what an odd thing
    to do…

T stands for *Tephromancy,*
    divination by ashes

    "ashes to ashes,
    dust to dust;
    the thing to look for on a poet
    is fust-
    ian."

O stands for *Oscitation,*
    what may happen if
    surrounded by too many Republican
        Californians
    fornicating cataphysically

N stands for *Neossine*,
    the substance of which
    the most edible poems in the West
    are made from,
    being a mucous secretion
    of the salivary glands
    of a genus of
    Broughtonian Angels

IV. SCUMBAGS FROM PARNASSUS

Headlines & Gorilla Hash Hot from the Helicon Herald

Our Fellow Murkins get the straight shit straight from AM Radio, CNN, Pat Robertson, Rush, Geraldo, Oprah, MTV, TedTurnerVision, and their papers of record: the tabloids by the checkout counters at Kroger, Harris Teeter, and Bi-Lo. *The National Enquirer* is becoming almost respectable, as standards for Nature, Man, and God plummet hourly.

"Scumbags from Parnassus" is an exercise in consanguinity, in belonging to the Bloody-Main-Greedy-Stream. I.e., IF YOU CAN'T CONJOIN THEM, CONFOUND THEM!

BOY WHORE CONDUCTS BOSTON SYMPHONY ORCHESTRA

INDUSTRIAL-STRENGTH LESBIANS DESTROY HALF OF SOUTH CAROLINA!!!

I WAS

HITLER'S

ASSHOLE!!!

NANCY:

"TOGETHER
WE CAN LICK
CRACK"

"DIRTY-DADDY DAY-CARE CENTERS" OPEN NATION-WIDE FRANCHISES

THEY'VE GOT THE BOMB— AND THEY'RE BLACK!!!

LIMBAUGH IN LIMBO—

RUSH RIMS BIMBOY!!!

FLUSH ONE BOX OF

RID-X DOWN JESSE

ALEXANDER HELMS JR. AND

WATCH HIM CHANGE INTO

A SENSITIVE CHARISMATIC

CHRISTIAN PERSON!!!

I'M BUYIN' THE COMPANY!!!

AMERICA'S
NAME IS
CHANGED TO
MURKA!
ONLY 3.9% OF POST-
GRADUATES CAN
SPELL EITHER

GOD GETS

THE JANITOR'S

JOB AT GRACELAND

AS ELVIS

TAKES

COMMAND OF

PLANET EARTH!!!

V. BUGTUSSLE

BEA HENSLEY HAMMERS AN IRON CHINQUAPIN LEAF ON
HIS ANVIL NEAR SPRUCE PINE, NORTH CAROLINA, & HE
COGITATES ON THE NATURE OF TWO BEAUTY SPOTS

in the Linville Gorge I
know this place

now it's a rock wall
you look up
it's covered in punktatum all
the way to Heaven

that's a
sight!

— ◦ —

up on Smoky
you ease up at daybust
and see the first
light in the tops of the tulip trees

now boys that just naturally
grinds and polishes
the soul

makes it
normal
again

I mean it's really
pretty!

UNCLE IV SURVEYS HIS DOMAIN FROM HIS ROCKER OF A SUNDAY AFTERNOON AS AUNT DORY STARTS TO CHOP THE KINDLIN

Mister Williams
lets youn me move
tother side the house

the woman
choppin wood's
mite nigh the awkerdist thing
I seen

THE AUTOCHTHON

if it was Clinch Valley, Virginia,
you'd figure:
James Stephens
was a Melungeon,

some kin to the famous Morning Glory Finch,
half-Indian/half-Raleigh's-Eden,
gone back to
ground...

but this is Newton County,
Arkansas Ozarks —
place with overhill towns
name of Parthenon, Ben Hur, Red Star,
Yellville, Verona, Snowball...

James Stephens lives in the woods:
one billy goat, two dogs, assorted ents,
one black cat

he plays the concertina for them
late at night
in women's clothes...

"You Are My Sunshine"—
contra natura

he often misses his dinner
that they may eat

"You Are My Sunshine"—
contra natura

on the table,
along with these photographs by Cherel Winett,
is an epigram
by Edward Dahlberg:

"I abhor the cult of the same that is the universal malady today,
and acknowledge I'm different, since I came into the world
like the four elements:
emotion, strife, remorse and chagrin."

I'd like to see James Stephens take a picture of Richard Nixon,
or Richard Avedon, from back in there where those eyes of his are—
a place, with topsoil in the character

the face
looks like J. Paul Getty
without a dime,
with character

the last face I saw anywhere near its equal,
that was Clarence Schmidt's, he
was sitting in the derelict car in the Wonder-Garden
on the Ohayo Ridge near Woodstock:

"call me Clarence, boys!
you from some sort of foundation?
—no, no use writing a poem, NBC's already did it,
screened it all over California…
bad thing too—these hippies come,
steal me blind…

yes, well, help yourselves, I got to fix thishere foil icicle
tree, see..."

like Ol' Man Turley Pickleseimer,
who hid out from the Guvmint during some war
in a cave down in Blue Valley,
which became known as "Pickleseimer Rock House,"
I hope James Stephens stays hid,
plays his goat-songs,
stays off TV and out of Fort Smith

as you know, Stephen Sykes,
of Aberdeen, Mississippi,
made the mistake of going into Memphis one night and later
remarked:

"Don't talk so much.
Keep your mouth
closed
and your bowels
open,

and believe in
Jesus!"

SYLLABLES IN THE FORM OF LEAVES

I

Fox plus *Razor* equals
the *Eye* —

get sharp,
or you're dead

II

Der Lenz kommt über Nacht, sagt
Li Po to

callow pussy
willows

III

Das Leben kann allerdings angesehen werden als ein Traum, a
succubus mused,
                            sliding down my private
waterfall

IV

Ein Vogel singt im Baum — Ja...
*Ja...*a

bud said,
swelling

v

Flogged with a *februum,*
young goats
dance out of

old goat skins

vi

Skin back the year,
turn over,
            you new leaf,
ewe!

THE MIDNITE SHOW

Red-Wigglers, Night-Crawlers
& Other Worms
look out
into the crapulous moonlight:

figures of women cascading through the Sunday night;

no beer in sight.

I remember the *Night-blooming*
Cereus by Dr. Thornton, Engraver, Blake's
patron, it
hangs in the hall outside the bedroom
swaying hungrily like these
giant white goddesses of the dark grotto...

there are touring cars
and men with large guns
singing through the woods

behind us.

THE ANCHORITE

quotes Basil Bunting from "Chomei at Toyama":
If you keep straight you will have no friends
but catgut and blossom in season.

the anchorite
opts to eye the
oak leaf, clutch
a red
to hold the mountains' blues
under the winter sun...

song accumulates heat — a humus. I have it,
like Issa:

> *Few people;*
> *a leaf falls here,*
> *falls there*

>   — outside, where
> the world's a storm
> in the oaks

> and the outcry of certain
> beautiful captures

—◦∾—

he wrote "brought to love," brought to any
intimacy,
            writing letters
among red oak leaves...

to be left alone? — that's a laugh! that is, who's
without the images of
love,
            shining out of his head?

and they
who move the heart, daringly,
as the sun fires the oak
through the wanton afternoon

—⚭—

light airs of music...

we are left with
just the "facts," the endless

articulation

A SPIN

I cut the stuff,
a whole blue field: figwort
's what they call it

this particular day I put a car through it,
very fast,
out the gate, second gear, sharp right —

right out of ourselves also say,
a few miles only, but

quite out, and up:

Highest Point East of South Dakota, it said:
6,684 feet,
oldest mountain on earth, etc.,
for what's in that

What good is a mountain without people? was all
he could ask

sure, it's what I mean —
if not, to hell with it!
I can, he said, regain composures,
and not only there...

The sun, suddenly hot on my hands,
holding the steering wheel;
the shadow of two ravens quickly across the car,
a dead raccoon by the road...

There are other things, I said, besides, say, air,
which, ok, you have to breathe, ok,
so also you gotta eat—like light or space,
or a mountain, very much,

which, if you'd climb the highest, works
well

SOME SOUTHPAW PITCHING
a riff for Charles Olson via Charles Ives

"let the song lie in the thing!" there's
music in anything! anything?

o there's poetry
in Mississippi; *exempli gratia,* the Iuka Drive-In:

I PASSED FOR WHITE plus
SNOW WHITE AND THE SEVEN SHADES

agreed?

Ives pitched for Hopkins Prep and beat
the Yale Freshmen and maybe pitched for Yale and beat
Dartmouth

once he stood in Dartmouth Common by the bon-fire
and heard the Glee-Club sing
"Where O Where Are the Pea-Green Freshmen?"

Ives, who knew how to take a lot off his knuckler,
took a lot off the tune, turning it
into the "Allegro" of the *Symphony #2* —
and Dvořák can't beat it

so, let the song lie in the ear, if it
hears it

where o where are the pea-green freshmen
d'antan?

even Helen Trent has gone to hell
in a boat,

where we all float—

or don't

The Shade of Ezra Pound once appeared to Charles Olson and uttered the poem's vatic first line. No one has quite understood what he meant, but it sounds like Heraclitus.

148

RUGGLES' VISIONARY SPECTRE IN VERMONT

spoke its bit from
Blake:
> *Great things are done when Men & Mountains meet*
> *This is not done by Jostling in the Street*

see page 661, Centenary Edition, where Will
also celebrates

     an Ass,
     a Hog,
     a Worm,
     a Chair,
     a Stool
— clearly the preferential

        if one be Artist in
        the reign of

        Crippled Harry & Slobbering Joe!!!

that new sound was 1949 — Nature (the Wilde One)
imitates Art again...

the *Organum* of Ruggles and Carl Ruggles walks
out of the hills into
Carnegie's Hall

        (the urbane sit on their
        hands
        hoping for Benjamin
        Britten)

I think he walked all the way from Arlington, Vermont,
across invisible mountains
to take that unseen bow
with Leopold Stokowski

and how *nobody*
knew this

it is to sound
such unknown men
I write —
      albeit this act but
      jostles in the Modern Street,

      a rude distraction

FIVE TRAIL-SHELTERS FROM THE
BIG PIGEON TO THE LITTLE TENNESSEE

1. *Davenport Gap*

the tulip poplar is not a
poplar it is a magnolia:
Liriodendron tulipifera.

the young grove on the eastern slopes of
Mt. Cammerer reminds me
of the two huge trees
at Monticello, favorites
of Mr. Jefferson;

and of the Virginia lady
quoting Mr. Kennedy:

the recent gathering of
Nobel Prize Winners at the
White House — the most
brilliant assemblage
in that dining room
since Mr. Jefferson
dined there

alone...

a liriodendron
wind, a liriodendron
mind

II. *Cosby Knob*

DeWitt Clinton (besides
looking like Lon
Chaney on tobacco-tax stamps)
comes to the eye
in *Clintonia borealis*—

of which fair green lily
there are millions
on this mountain,

it is a mantle
for fire-cherry, yellow birch,
and silver bell

III. *Tri-Corner Knob*

here the shelter's
in a stand of
red spruce and balsam fir

for dinner: lamb's-quarters,
cress from the streams
on Mt. Guyot,
wood sorrel, and
cold argentine beef, chased with
tangerine kool-aid

IV. *False Gap*

no *Schwarzwald* stuff,
keine Waldeinsamkeit,

no magic grouse, no
Brothers Grimm — just
Canadian hemlock, mossed and lichened,
like unto maybe
Tertiary time…

too much for a haiku?
you hike it and see

V. *Silers Bald*

just in front of the
round iron john
in the beech grove

the fresh bear droppings
give you

something
to think about

PAEAN TO DVOŘÁK, DEEMER & McCLURE

besides Beethoven and Brahms, Dvořák "studied
with the birds, flowers, trees, God, and
himself"

VHOOR ZHOCK!
VHOOR ZHOCK!
VHOOR ZHOCK!

I celebrate this Slavic creature
who so sang and loved America at a time
Henry James, Gent.,
went around in a closed railroad car in Georgia lamenting
nobody cared, nobody cared, how dreary
the land was and
always would be...

1893, June: Spillville, Iowa:
the *F major Quartet,* "The American" (Opus 96),
composed in three days (!) in a village
composed of Czech immigrants and many
birds on the Turkey River

"a damned bird (red, only with black wings)" sang its way
into the *Scherzo*
and stayed there

(Spillville is between
Eldorado and Jerico
west of
US 52)

On the Continent the Quartet is called
"The Nigger Quartet"—

Ach, Meinen Damen und Herren, it was a
red bird not a black bird,
and your version of America is, as usual, absurd…

however, other ears were hearing the American land,
particularly, Mr. Charles Ives's…

he, as Lou Harrison says, "decomposed" the demotic and found
music in the ground

but Dvořák took to the aire, his drone is the hive of melody
of a Bohemian's yearning, his discerning
of the American Grain Eden—
mellifluous and glorious, sad, sweet, strong—sung so
in the *Cello Concerto*
"Praise is the practice of art!"

WOOD/BIRD/GOD/WORD
HEARD WORLD!

—⚬—

my god I'd like to go to bed with everybody,
even with the chickens and with the moon and get up
like a sun!

let's all go to Oregon and eat
yard eggs, drink home-churned whole
buttermilk in stone crocks, bake
bread of whole-wheat flour—

and may orchards and rivers
ease us!

——◦——

O Grass of Parnassus,
where have we been
(the bottle gentian
and I) all
your life?

*"now I am ice, now
I am sorrel"*—

Thoreau, clear as springwater, cog-wheel nature
fitted into the infinite
under his foot...

wool plus lichen plus human urine make
black tweed

so we take the Golden Road, the Road
to the Palace of Wisdom, we take the Walk
to the Paradise Garden

intent upon sorrel
like Angelico and Botticelli and
fertilized
by the smaller bees and flies...

Delius tells us, Blake tells us, the lake, the
catbird, the oak gall, the aspen, the plantain, the weed,
seed, jugs, clouds, fires,
thrones, thorns, mires, snakes
tell us:

We are the Ruination
& the Light!

it is simple-minded to say so,
it is single-minded to say so —
we ask to be close to those
who are lost here, they are our kinsmen:
lichen
alga
and *granite*...

work for the night is coming,
work for the night is coming,
work for the night is coming,
when man's work is done...

— Charles Ives worked that corny presbyterian hymn tune
into nearly every piece he wrote

you rust out or
you burn out

and if this be the last night,
let it be! see
how few
will grieve us:

alga?
lichen?
granite?

I have asked the wood thrush to bless us:

philos!
philos!
philos!

SYMBIOSIS WE PRAY!
SYMBIOSIS WE PRAY!
SYMBIOSIS WE PRAY!

CURIOSITIES OF ALE & BEER FROM
THE BICKERDYKE CHRONICLE

The Uneuphonious White-Ale of Cornwall:
laboragol

Quoting Pope, "The Clamorous Crowd Is Hushed With Mugs of:
mum"

In Vogue with the Roystering Blades of Former Times:
huff-cap

The Luscious Fluid Producing the Bloated Habit of Body of the
West-Country Connoisseur, Bones Phillips:
grout

An Ale Consumed With Gusto in Cymru:
cwrwf

The Beer of Barley, Cambridgeshire, That "Won't Let the People Go":
Pharaoh

Drunk in the Country on Mothering Sunday:
bragot

A somewhat Remote Ancestor of Ruddle:
dogsnose

The Wassail of November First, Sacred to the Angel That Presides
Over Fruits & Seeds, "La Mas Ubal":
Lambswool

The Very Writing of This Word Summons Visions of a Shining River, of Shady Backwaters, of Summer Days, of Two-Handled Tankards, of Deep, Cool Draughts:
shandy-gaff

Composed of Equal Proportions of "Old & Bitter":
mother-in-law

Roman Wormwood, Gentian Root, Calamus Aromaticus, Snake Root, Horse Radish, Dried Orange Peel, Juniper Berries, Kernels of Seville Oranges, All Placed in Beer, Plus a Pound of Galingale for Taste, Become the Sublime:
purl

Of the Greatest Benefit in Incipient Consumption in 1744:
stitch

The Reputation for Being Most Excellent Tipple:
tewahdiddle

The Squeeze of the Crabs Growing in the Wild in the Woods (Appropriate to Nations Who Have Made But Slight Advances on the Path of Civilization):
cyder

EMBLEMS FOR THE LITTLE DELLS,
AND NOOKS, AND CORNERS OF PARADISE

out of the stills of Habersham: occasionally
potable calvados...

out of the hills of Habersham: sham
trochees, Ol' Marse Sidney's poses, Poe's
memories of the Lost Lenore, ah, Last of the Cherokee Queens, elas...

alas,
no one has *yet* seen the Soqui River in Habersham County, Georgia
(not far from Lake Lanier), on a winter afternoon between the hills —

no one except its despisers, versifiers, fishers, hunters, dumpers
of inner tubes, runners of sugar liquor, and errant crackers,
who are
familiar Christian white folks with
red necks and blue
noses,

brown mule and
black hearts...

it is hard to see the Soqui River in the late red sun
of a December afternoon (I reckon not
even Henry James saw it) —
it is too hard to attune to, or atone for;

it is a stone's throw across that dark water to
Secure, Literary Yesteryear: Palmer
speaking of "that 'stinking hole Shoreham' which indeed is now
highly scented with the buds of spring"

...everywhere and forever more everything's stinking, but thanks
for thinking of us, Sam,
standing there staring into the sun

with the apple trees sizzling and the valley yelling FIRE,
for we are not troubled by problems of aerial perspective in
the Valley of Vision—

> Zion is in the Sun
> of England's
> Eden
> on the Darenth,
> Kent

and we can turn it into the moon of Bunyan's Beulah Land and
hear the Voice of the Bard:

"the green mountains that glimmer in a summer gloaming
from the dusky yet bloomy east;

the moon opening her golden eye, or walking in brightness
among innumerable islands of light,
not only thrill the optic nerve but shed
a mild,
a grateful,
an unearthly lustre
into the inmost spirits,
and seem the interchanging twilight
of that peaceful country

where there is no sorrow
and no night"

roll the apple away from the tomb, put
an apple in the mouth of Stinking Lazarus;

put it in the sky,
make a moon of it!

we are willing to raise anything!

the nightingale is singing
on Hampstead Heath
141 years after the death
of Keats

tradition is in us
like the sun

"sin is
separation"

The poem begins as a parody of Lanier's "Song of the Chattahoochee," a ubiquitous bit of nineteenth-century fluff... Blake once wrote to his young disciple Samuel Palmer about the business of poetry: "You have only to work up imagination to that state of vision and the thing is done."

DILMUS HALL, WHO ASSURES US HE'S BEEN RIGHT
HERE IN THE FLESH FOR ABOUT 4,004 YEARS, ONE WAY
OR ANOTHER, AND HASN'T BATHED ONCE,
DELIVERS SOME GOSPEL:

you have eyes
outside
and eyes
inside

your heart
is full
of eyes

to communicate
you put the two
together

amen!

FROM UNCLE JAKE CARPENTER'S ANTHOLOGY
OF DEATH ON THREE-MILE CREEK

Loney Ollis
age 84
dide jun 10 1871

grates dere honter
wreked bee trees for hony
cild ratell snak by 100
cild dere by thousen

i nod him well

DEALER'S CHOICE AND THE DEALER SHUFFLES
for William Burroughs

I saw the Chattahoochee River get a haircut.
I saw Fidel Castro flow softly toward Apalachicola, Florida.

I saw a bank of red clay integrate with Jesuits.
I saw Bob Jones Bible University used to make baked flamingos.

I saw the Governor of Mississippi join the NAACP.
I saw a black gum tree refuse to leaf and go to jail.

I saw the DAR singing "We Shall Overcome"!
I saw Werner von Braun knitting gray (and brown) socks for the
          National Guard.

I saw the Motto of Alabama: "IT'S TOO WET TO PLOUGH!"
I saw God tell Adam: "WE DARE DEFEND OUR RIGHTS!"

I saw the City of Albany fried in deep fat.
I saw eight catfish star on Gomorrah TV.

I saw *The Invasion of the Body Snatchers* at the Tyger Drive-In.
I saw William Blake grow like a virus in the sun.

I saw the South suckin hind titty.
I saw the North suckin hind titty.

I saw a man who saw these too.
And said though strange they were all true.

Postface: *"There was a crow sat on a clod—*
          And now I've finished my sermon, thank God."

A ROUND OF NOUNS IN JACKSON COUNTY

Rough Butt Creek
to
Bearwallow Fork
to
Snaggy Bald
to
Mayapple Gap
to
Fern Mountain
to
Soapstone Gap
to
Rocky Face Cliff
to
Alum Knob
to
John Brown Branch
to
Hornyhead Mountain
to
Niggerskull Mountain
to
Sugar Creek Gap
to
Rough Butt Creek

THE LOOKOUT TOWER AT MOUNT VENUS, LOUISIANA

yes yes O Lord yes the bestest sweetest
pussy
     ever said good-morning to a slop jar...

you know:
         "nappy" pussy,
like counting
prayer beads:

. . . . ( ) . . . .

Heard-object from Clement, man-servant to Weeks Hall, Esq., at the latter's plantation,
Shadows-on-the-Teche, New Iberia, Louisiana, 1957.

FREE ADMISSION REPTILE GARDEN

the mind is, or might be,
                                   a rattle, or
nest of,
        hung on the tail
of some snake
                 (parading dangerous, dull phlegm,
only…)

so assumed, it whirs through a shimmer of an inspired
piss off a tinplate,

and it struts dins blares
the wild farrago

and/or it leadeth into temptation, and
I shall not want
it,

   particularly

EPITAPHS FOR TWO NEIGHBORS IN MACON COUNTY
NO POET COULD FORGET

Uncle Iv Owens

he done
what he could
when he got round
to it

Aunt Dory Owens

always
dahlies

always

THE CUSTODIAN OF A FIELD OF WHISKEY BUSHES
BY THE NOLICHUCKY RIVER SPEAKS:

took me a pecka real ripe tomaters up
into the Grassy Gap
one night

and two quarts of good stockade
and just laid there

sippin and tastin and lookin agin the moon
at them sorta fish eyes in the jar
you get when its right

boys Im talkin bout somethin
good!

A CHORALE* OF CHEROKEE NIGHT MUSIC AS HEARD
THROUGH AN OPEN WINDOW IN SUMMER LONG AGO

wahuhu wahuhu wahuhu wahuho wahuhu wahuhu w
uku uguko uguko uguku uguku uguku uguku uguk u
u huhu huhu htuhu htuhu huhu hubu huhu huhu hu
lu lalu lalu lalu lalu lalu lalu lalu lalu lalu lalu lalu lalu lalu
latu talatu talatu talatu talatu talatu talatu talatu talatu tal
lili tsikilili tsikilili tsikilili tsikilili tsikil tsikil tsikil tsikil ts
ikiki tsikiki tsikiki tsikiki tsikiki tsikiki tsikiki tsikiki ts
u kagu kagu kagu kagu kagu kagu kagu kagu kagu kag
ya waya waya waya waya waya waya waya waya waya
ah yeah yeah yeah yeah yeah yeah yeah yeah yeah ye
a guna guna guna guna guna guna guna guna guna guna
sasa sasa sasa sas a sasa sass sass sasa sasa sasa sasa sasa s
unu kununu kununu kununu kununu kununu kunun
stu dustu dustu dustu dustu dustu dustu dustu dus

---

*screech owl
hoot owl
yellow-breasted chat
jar-fly
cricket
carolina chickadee
katydid
crow
wolf
beetle
turkey
goose
bullfrog
spring frog

EDDIE OWENS MARTIN, ST. EOM,
LEAVES MARION COUNTY, GEORGIA,
THE SECOND AND FINAL TIME,
APRIL 16, 1986

bewna vista was on
the main southern passenger line to florida

i used to stand in the weeds longside the tracks
and look at all those fine people
eating and drinking behind thick glass
in the dining car

my my

when i was 14
i told my brutal old daddy
to fuck himself
i told marion county georgia
to fuck itself
i went to the department store
bought me some long pants
hopped a freight north
ended up on manhattan island
and headed right for 42nd street

man i never looked back

HOJOKI

no loot, no
lust to string a catgut
in a banjo

to hoot
or holler into
Nawth Jawja

too effete to
chant "Chattahoochee"
in trochaic feet

all's quiet at
Hut City

I have, in fact, stayed at length at a hermitage in Habersham County, Georgia, overlooking the rock upon which Mr. Sidney Lanier allegedly wrote his tedious, famous poem. This eyrie on Tray Mountain was larger than Chomei's "ten-foot-square hut," but I imagine quieter.

LAMENTS FROM THE PIGEON ROOST NEWS

once we all grew shellet
potato onions everybody
around here have run out of
seed E.E. Seaton
of Jonesboro
Tennessee done heard
about this

—⟡—

the Fourth-a-July
Holiday
passed off in this part
very quiet

—⟡—

that snake were such
peculiar looking
to me I'm afraid I
couldn't give it justice
trying to describing it but it
didn't act mean like
it tryed to be
pretty like
it did

A RIDE IN A BLUE CHEVY FROM ALUM CAVE TRAIL
TO NEWFOUND GAP

goin' hikin'?
git in!

o the Smokies are ok but me
I go for Theosophy,
higher things, Hindu-type philosophy,
none of this licker and sex, I
like it
on what we call the astral plane,
I reckon I get more i-thridral
by the hour

buddy, you won't believe this but
how old you reckon the earth is?
the earth is
precisely 156 trillion years old
I got this book from headquarters in
Wheaton, Illinois,
says it is!

I'll tell you somethin' else:
there are exactly 144 kinds of people on this earth,
12 signs and the signs change
every two hours,
that's 144, I'm Scorpio,
with Mars over the water

here's somethin' else innerestin':
back 18 million years
people was only one sex, one sex only...
I'd like to explain that,
it's right here in this pamphlet,
50 cents...

never married, lived with my mother in Ohio,
she died, I'm over in Oak Ridge
in a machine shop, say,
what kind of place
is Denver?
think I'll sell this car, go to Denver,
set up a Center...

name's Davis,
what's yours?

THE ANCIENT OF DAYS

would that I
had known Aunt Cumi
Woody

C-u-m-i, pronounced
Q-my

she lived in the Deyton Bend Section of Mitchell
County, North Carolina, many years ago

there is one of Bayard Wootten's photographs of her
standing there with her store-bought
teeth, holding a coverlet

she sheared her sheep, spun
and dyed her yarn in vegetable dyes,
and wove the coverlet

in indigo, the brown from walnut roots,
red from madder, green from hickory ooze, first,
then into the indigo (the blue pot)

Cumi, from the Bible
(Saint Mark 5:41)

Talitha Cumi:
"Damsel, I say unto thee, arise!"

she is gone, she
enjoyed her days

OLD MAN SAM WARD'S HISTORY
OF THE GEE-HAW WHIMMY-DIDDLE

some folks say
the injuns made 'em
like lie-detectors
called 'em
hoodoo sticks

feller
in Salisbury, Noth Caylini,
made the first
whimmy-diddle I seen

I whittle seven
kind: thisuns king
size, thisuns jumbo, thisuns
extry large

here's a single, here's one
double, here's a triple and why right here
here's a forked 'un

been whittlin' whimmy-diddles come
ten year, I reckon you'd
care to see my other toys,
boys, I got some fine
flipper-dingers, fly-
killers and bull-roarers, I can

kill a big fly at sixty feet

watch here

THREE SAYINGS FROM HIGHLANDS, NORTH CAROLINA

but pretty though as
roses is
you can put up with
the thorns

Doris Talley, Housewife & Gardener

you live until you die —
if the limb don't fall

Butler Jenkins, Caretaker

your points is blue
and your timing's
a week off

Sam Creswell, My Auto Mechanic

SELECTED LISTINGS FROM THE WESTERN CAROLINA TELEPHONE COMPANY'S DIRECTORY (BRYSON CITY, CASHIERS, CHEROKEE-WHITTIER, CULLOWHEE, FRANKLIN, HIGHLANDS, SYLVA)

Applewhite Max
Bell Corydon
Chiltoshey Going Back Mrs
Cody Verlous
Cope Ode
Cox Plato
Crisp Gentry
Dalton Dock
Evitt Delphia Mrs
Flack Kolin
Foxx Zollie Rev
Game Gertrude
Gibson Pink
Good Colon L Rev
Gribble Geneva
Huggins Rass
Imperato Pat
Johnson John Bunion
Jones Vestal
Keen Yeoman
Keener Maiden
King Hill
Kiser Julian (Bug)
Love Jeter
Mashburn Angeline
Moss Floda

Muse O. U.
Norton Paschal
Orr Deaver
Owl Frell
Painter Fern
Peek Benlon
Pickens Excellent F
Picklesimer Turley
Polk James K.
Queen Kennith
Quiet Lily
Rainwater Veezey
Rogers Gas Island
Shook Troy
Sneed Cam
Strong Hope
Tweed Strang
Undergrowth Hom
Van Lyon
Ward Milas
Webb Zero
Whittle Chester
Wold Maude
Womack Kibby
Wood Cooter
Youngbird Rufus

ARLISS WATFORD OF WINTON, N.C.,
PRICES A TOTEM POLE IN A SELLING MOOD

let's see:
six of them
injun heads

i've got $75 worth of work
in each one of those
that's $420

the thunderbird design
that'll be $20

and the crown
on top
i'll throw it in
for $5

let's call it $450
and you get
the pole
for free

if you don't like that
i've got a
'29 A-Model
you can drive home
this very morning

you can steal it
from this poor citizen:
$7500

seventy-five hundred, seventy-five hundred…
my, my,
that's thievery

WOODROW GANTT
OF PELION, SOUTH CAROLINA
("PEANUT CAPITAL OF SOUTH CAROLINA"),
WHICH IS 14 MILES NORTH OF NORTH, SOUTH CAROLINA,
TELLS THAT:

> things were a-gettin' slow
> out here at the Po-
> Folks Horse Arena (every damnthing
> except the track's imaginary
> so you kin jest imagine
> hit gets old)
>
> so me and brother Dan
> decided to hold us
> a Men-Only Ugly Contest
>
> trouble was
> a bunch of folks what weren't ugly at all
> entered the thing
> last summer
> just to get 'em some
> prize money
>
> why no women?
> hellsfire there's no call
> to encourage women
> ugly as they already are
> in Lexington County!

AUNT DORY ELLIS, OF PENLAND,
REMEMBERS WHEN SHE FELL
IN HER GARDEN AT THE HOME PLACE
AND BROKE HER HIP IN 19 AND 56

the sky was high,
white clouds passing
by, I lay
a hour in that petunia patch

hollered,
and knew I was out of whack

THE HERMIT CACKLEBERRY BROWN, ON HUMAN VANITY

caint call your name
but your face is easy

come sit

now some folks figure theyre
bettern
cowflop they
aint

not a bit

just good to hold the world together
like hooved up ground

thats what

THE MAP OF KENTUCKY AND ITS LITANY
OF GLORIFICATION

Slap Out
Hi Hat
Pulltite
Sugartit

Pride
Pomp

Bliss
Pippa Passes
Sacred Wind

Lovely Pilgrim
Muses Mills
Humility
Rowdy
Decay
Poverty
Hoodoo
Tyewhoppety
Monkeys Eyebrow
Mummie
Viva
Kill Time
Chicken Bristle
Skullbuster
Ordinary
Marrowbone
Mouth of Beaver
Kingdom Come
Climax
Rough and Ready
Red Hot

Hot Spot
Ice
Uz

Uno
Ono
Slowgo
Glo
Kinniconick
Mouthcard
Ages
Wolf Coal
Beefhide
Hippo
Plank
Virgo
Cerulean
Sunfish
Pig
Zag
Lukewarm
Mousie
Wisdom
Summer Shade
Shoulder Blade
Hardshell
Hell for Certain
Power
Canoe
Nada
Egypt
South America

Korea
Dongola
Disputanta
Dwarf
Bee
Boreing
Bypro
Moon
Relief
Lair
Whippoorwill
Gravel Switch
Cranks
Kaliopi
Eskippakithiki
Possum Trot

Crum
Crocus

Hardmoney
Bugtussle
Turkeyfoot
Scuffletown
Waltz
Pebble
Smile
Wheel
Wax
Candy
Grab

Rabbit Hash
Habit
Rush
Static
Load
Acorn
Rightangle

Frog Level
Sunshine
Black Jack
Hail
Future City
Ready
Sideview
Soft Shell
Dice
Letter Box
Vortex

Black Snake

Neon
Ruin
Bagdad
Bee

Thousandsticks
Razorblade
Nuckles
Shytown
Gleanings
Butterfly
Trickum
Jugornot
Noble
Joy

Big Bone Lick
Head of Grassy

Arminta Ward's Bottom
Rains
Beauty

Awe
Stop

NIGHT LANDSCAPE IN NELSON COUNTY, KENTUCKY

ah, Moon, shine
thou as amber in thy
charred-keg, hickory sky...

still as a still, steep
as a horse's face

TOM MERTON'S NEIGHBOR, ANDY BOONE, LOOKS UP

Father,

when the wild turkeys
fly south
and say

W

A

R

with their wings,

it's liable to be
war

CARVING A FEW PINE LINES
WITH CARL McKENZIE UP SNAKY HOLLER,
NADA, KENTUCKY

how old are you
Carl

i'm 50 years old
not counting
the 34 years
i went barefoot

have you been
carving much

not much boys
i'm about carved out
been whittlin' on
this bird for a week
and just makin'
shavins

i was at the cemetery just yesterday
and it just about tore me up
seein' edna's name on that stone

of course
if i heared of a widow woman
with a lotta money
and a bad cough
i might just do it one more time

JOHN CHAPMAN PULLS OFF THE HIGHWAY
TOWARD KENTUCKY AND CASTS A COLD EYE
ON THE MOST ASTONISHING SIGN
IN RECENT AMERICAN LETTERS:

O'NAN'S

AUTO

SERVICE

LEE OGLE TIES A BROOM &
PONDERS A CURE FOR ARTHURITIS

lands them fingers really
dreadfulled me I
couldnt tie
nary broom one

had to soak em in water
hot as birds blood

then I heared this ol' man from Kentucky say
take a jug of apple juice just juice not cider
pour the epsum salts to it and
take as much as you kin

bein fleshy I kin take
right smart but
boys you know it moves a mans bowels
somethin terrible

well boys it just
naturally killed that arthuritis
lost me some weight too
and I
still tie thesehyar brooms

pretty good

COUSIN POEMS

Dicky

slimy,
like his daddy

—☙—

Randy

likes to
kill things

very nice
to his mama

—☙—

Maude

all those years,
married to Doyle

—☙—

Libba

the interesting one,
married a Jew man,
did herself in

—☙—

Carl

liked to color
his nails

became
a barber

—☙—

Janet

strange as
they come

a stone
with a skin

—☙—

Harold

instead of a
mind

a room
empty

save for
a Gideon Bible

hiding
a snake

THREE (MAKE IT FOUR) TAVERN SONGS IN THE LATE SOUTHERN T'ANG MANNER

I. *Trunkene im Frühling (My Version)*

or—who else go into the shrubbery
muttering

or shine the silver flashlight
at the female dormitory,
longingly?

        questions, questions…always
        constrictions—

                ah, to sit
                in the catbird seat

II. *Again the Night*

so the moon, as she rose
red,
    swung clean, from the hill,

but her face through the window had "Heart of Kentucky" on it, an
obfuscation (always a mystery), a
sour mash,

       like this typewriter
crashing across the swamp grass,
as if brushing it
aside…

and trees, goddamn everywhere,
and figures of speech!

III. *The Desperado*

so,
a bottle of bourbon on the top shelf, why
not?

or,
who are you, you
yankee, to ask *anything*?

you've been seeing too many drive-in movies;
that is,
nobody does,
in fact
here
drink—

only ice water, or
syllabub, sometimes,

in the gloaming,
tra la

IV. *Die Farbe ist Eine Figur*

twere i more the painter
twould be cool to register

the fields of asters,
joe-pye, ironweeds, and shastas

than hotrod thru the goldenrod, faster,
into nearby georgia for ice-cold buds

"The catbird seat" is an expression popularized by the sports announcer Red Barber: a cat
bird invariably perches in the topmost branch of a tree—very securely so. Heart of
Kentucky is a popular brand of bourbon whiskey. Syllabub, originally, is an English con-
coction of goat's milk and white wine.

DADDY BOSTAIN, THE MOSES OF THE WING COMMUNITY MOONSHINERS, LAMENTS FROM HIS DEATHBED THE SPIRITUAL ESTATE OF ONE OF HIS SOUL-SAVING NEIGHBORS

God bless her pore
little ol'
dried up
soul!

jest make
good kindlin wood
fer Hell...

THE MEDITATIONS OF POLICE CHIEF MARIO BALZIC

an irish intellectual
in the white house
a fucking a-rab loony
in a tent

forget it!

—◎—

if pete rose
is 45

I must be
dead

—◎—

the legs get whiter
and the gut
hangs over...

—◎—

main floor
any downtown office tower
all the johns are locked
you sneak around behind the newsstand
and pray god it's
just a fart

—◎—

one day
after another

THORNTON DIAL TALKS ABOUT
EVERY FACE IN AMERICA,
HIS NEW, LARGE PAINTING

there they are
every face in america

every white face every black face
every brown face every red face
every yellow face

there are all the animals
you can't kill animals in america they safe
you can't kill no animals in america —
until you buy a license

you can't kill no fish either in america —
until you buy a license

against the law to kill black people
brown people red people yellow people —
no need to do that

what you do is put them all on welfare —
that's all you need to do

all that ham and fat bacon
from the company store
that does it
slow maybe but
it does it

frozen chitlins
that does it
it's real easy

frozen chitlins
that's the diet
for dead niggers

THREE THEFTS FROM JOHN EHLE'S PROSE

every night
the possums climb higher
in the persimmon trees

—◦◦—

a red pumpkin
in a row of yellow pumpkins
in a field

—◦◦—

better'n
a creek
fulla syrup

MRS. SADIE GRINDSTAFF, WEAVER & FACTOTUM, EXPLAINS THE WORK-PRINCIPLE TO THE MODERN WORLD

I figured
anything anybody
could do a lot of I
could do a little
of

mebby

AUNT CREASY, ON WORK

shucks
I make the livin

uncle
just makes the livin
worthwhile

SNUFFY SMITH'S COLOSSAL MAW
FROM WAR-WOMAN DELL

more mouth on
that woman

than ass
on a goose

THE EPITAPH ON UNCLE NICK GRINDSTAFF'S GRAVE
ON THE IRON MOUNTAIN ABOVE
SHADY VALLEY, TENNESSEE

LIVED ALONE

SUFFERED ALONE

DIED ALONE

VI. NUDE DRIVER THREW LARD!

FOUND POEM NUMBER ONE:
(Fifth General Hospital, Bad Cannstatt/Stuttgart, 1953: the speaker, a
bop spade from Cleveland in a fugue state, making the world's first
marriage of the poetics of Charles Olson and Dame Edith Sitwell—
and you are there!)

man,
i come from
the 544
   motherfuckin'
      double-clutchin'
         cocksuckin'
           truckin' company!

U CALL—
WE HAUL
U ALL...

we got
2 plys
  4 plys
    6 plys
      8 plys, semi's—

and them BIG motherfuckers
go

CHEW!
CHEW

NUDE DRIVER THREW LARD

associated press tifton georgia
a tifton man has
been convicted of public
indecency and placed on
probation for slinging chunks
of lard at women
while driving a car
in the nude tommy
st john 31 was
arrested last monday after
a car chase by
officers investigating the latest
escapade of the assailant
who has been dubbed
the crisco kid crisco
is a brand of
store-bought lard-like vegetable shortening

POSTCARD OF SEPTEMBER 12, 1936, TO MISS LEHMAN OF CINCINNATI FROM THE WESTSIDE YMCA, NEW YORK CITY

Dear Mary Jo,
just arrived.

Jim met me
at the train.

We are taking
a double-room here.

Love, Larry.

SCRAWLED UNDER THE M-56 BRIDGE, PRESTON BROOK

Mrs Lot
has a salty twot

AND NOW FOR A MESSAGE
FOR DRIVERS IN CAMBRIDGE
(FROM RADIO 4)

an abnormal load
is about to leave
Caxton Gibbet…

—❦—

We Interrupt These Texts to Bring You a News Flash
from the Times of London, June 6, 1972:

"IN MID-MORNING AN ELDERLY LADY WHOSE LUGGAGE
  WAS BEING SEARCHED SUDDENLY SHOUTED:
  'KEEP YOUR HANDS OFF MY KIPPERS, YOUNG MAN!' HER
  VOICE ECHOED ROUND THE DEPARTURE LOUNGE AND
  SCARED OTHER PASSENGERS. WHEN ASSURED THAT
  HER KIPPERS WOULD REMAIN SACROSANCT
  SHE APOLOGIZED."

CARTE DE VISITE D'AMANDA McKITTRICK ROS
(THE GREATEST BAD WRITER IN THE WORLD)

"always at home
  to the Very Great"

THE GOZ

flitting about
like a half-frigged
fly…

PROCLAMATIONS ON TIN IN THE GARDEN OF
MARY TILLMAN SMITH

A DOG BARK & MOTHER AROUND LOOK OUT

I WAS IN A RAKE THE LORD WAS FOR ME

I DONT NO NO BIT

HERE IS 1980 TIM GON BY

THE OLD COTSWOLD FIRM OF GROIN GROCERS:

EROS BROS GROS GLOS

A SIGN IN THE LUNE VALLEY REVEALS
"THE WAY OF THE TRIFFIDS":

HEAVY PLANT CROSSING

IN INGLETON THE EYE CONTEMPLATES
THE SIGN OF A FIRM OF SOLICITORS:

GOAD & BUTCHER

SHIT HAPPENS!

—Heraclitean bumper-sticker, New Orleans…

DOO-DOO HAPPENS

—Simpering, mealy-mouthed bumper-sticker, Atlanta

EXCREMENT OCCURS, POSSIBLY

—Imaginary bumper-sticker, London

———⊙∽———

PHILIP HOPE-WALLACE (1911–1979)

Gentlemen I must
report from a visit
to Lesbos

the natives are Lesbians
to a man

G.B.S.: "LE PENSEUR"
for Alvin Langdon Coburn

"hundreds of
photographs of
Dickens and
Wagner…

we see
nothing
of them
except their suits
of clothes
with their heads
sticking out;

and what is
the use
of that?"

POETRY IN PRINT, A MONTHLY REVIEW

"iambics

so resolutely symmetrical
that reading them

is like being kicked in the head
by an absentminded
boy scout"

ON THE STONE OF AARON ISSACS, EASTHAMPTON

An Israelite,

in whom
there was
no guile...

VICTORIA WOOD, IN *TALENT:*

I always thought
coq au vin

was
love in a lorry

THE FIVE WORST NAMES OF BOATS MOORED
ON THE BRIDGEWATER CANAL

Floating Pound
Sai Wen
Me.and.Er
Dawn Treader
Tribulation

SIGN IN A GARDEN IN COUNTY CORK

LADIES & GENTLEMEN WILL NOT

AND OTHERS MUST NOT

PULL THE FLOWERS IN THIS GARDEN

IN THE GREEN GROCER'S WINDOW, BATH

THE PENALTIES

FOR SHOPLIFTING

ARE EXTREMELY HIGH

THE PUBLICITY

HARMFUL

THE YORKSHIRE ANTI-RIPPER PROCEDURAL KIT

"swing your handbags, rake
his shins with stiletto heels, knee
him in the groin,
bite and scratch him, and
scream"

if he's not the Ripper,
he might become so

THE LAVATORIES OF STOCKPORT, LANCASHIRE

others convicted
include a
barrister, a Manchester
magistrate, a
credit control worker, a
lecturer, a
chemical process worker, a
heavy goods driver, a
telephone engineer, and a
driving school proprietor…

A SERIES OF FIVE CHARRED, BLACKENED LUMPS
SERVED AS "MIXED GRILL"
BY THE HIGH FORCE HOTEL,
UPPER TEESDALE, COUNTY DURHAM

From the Shapes, Please Tell Us Which Are:

(1)   the Sausage
(2)   the Lamb Chop
(3)   the Mushroom
(4)   the Tomato
(5)   the Kidney

OWJADOO

Yorkshireman
went into a Jermyn Street
hat shop

whipper-snapper clerk
snipped out real poshlike
And what
is your pleasure
sir?

Yorkshireman
said back
Fookin' an' pigeons
but whut ahm wahntin'
reet naow
izza flat 'at

sonnie

A SEBBER QUARTET

I

R.F.T.
"Robbie" Thislethwaite
ANTIQUARIAN BOOKSELLERS ASSOCIATION,
it says in the window

he gives no impression of
ever having read a book in his life
except for the high prices
in catalogues
from London auctions,
those he reads

cuts a rare figure
sauntering along Main Street
in a toupee
that looks like
a 2p rug sample
stewed in
stale tea

the
stiffupperlip
alerts the
peasants
to his local
import

II

Hoggarth
the Chemist,

the C.B.E. after his name
stands for
Colossal Bore of the Empire

you want 100 aspirin
you get 25 minutes on
"Wartime Pharmacy
in the
British Zone
of Occupied Germany"

peek into his
black-leather-lined basement
on a
wet winter's night...

see the man himself
in High-Nazi kit,
doing an appalling
goose step,
working on
the big spiel
about Der Führer
about how he really had some jolly good ideas,
mate,

for Nignog England,
now!

III

Uncle Tot Harper
could talk
the tits
off a hog

farmed sheep
fifty years
under Crook
under Winder
and's done
nowt since
but natter

get
the good man
a gob-stopper
for Christmas

reminds me
Miss Stein said Mr. Pound
was a village explainer

ok if you're a village;
if not, not

IV

"Mad Dick"
pumps petrol
on the forecourt
at
SEDBERGH MOTOR CO. LTD

being worth
nowt
but nine pence
in the bob
one assumes
he's paid
two Mars Bars
in the morning,
two Mars Bars
in the afternoon…

nights,
occupies a disused bunker
built on the River Rawthey
in the times
of Hitler's War,
sips
chamomile tea

only person in Cumbria
who sings passages
of Sir Thomas Browne's
Hydriotaphia
quietly to himself
when moonlight pours
over Black Horse Hill

THE FAIRY FELLER'S MASTER-STROKE:

on the drink
Mad Dick Dadd
had a mad on
and half a hard-
on for Old Dad,
had
to hack Dad's
dick off
in Gravesend

in tendrils &
thistles
in Gravesend

the rhymes end
in tendrils &
thistles

in Bedlam,
in 1887

J. ATKINSON GRIMSHAW'S PAINTINGS AT LEEDS

"repellent
in their supine sentimentality
these Victorian visions
are still popular,"

proclaims Pamela
(Knée Jerk) Kirk

with alliteration & pig-ignorance
in today's *Guardian*
art pages

THOMAS JOHNES, MASTER OF HAFOD YCHDRYD
(THE SUMMER PALACE BY THE WINDING RIVER),
CARDIGANSHIRE/EDEN

it must look today very much as Johnes first saw it,
seventeen-whatever-it-was…

some son of a bitch has, recently, made a killing off the lead rights
and cut the last of Johnes's trees

between October 1795 and April 1801
he planted two million sixty-five thousand trees,
nearly half of them being larch

for, outside the Domain of Hafod, Wales was like this,
to quote a much later account (1854) by George Borrow:

"much mire in the street;
immense swine lay in the mire…
women in Welsh hats stood in the mire, along with men
without any hats"

hee hee
hoo hoo
said the locals

that is Borrow at the Bridge of the Holy Ford,
on the way to Strata Florida, Vale of Flowers,
where he kissed the Yew-Tree, sacred to Davidd Ab Gwilym,
one of the first poets of the world

the locals
are still
cackling

but, back, the first Hafod burned, 1807
(a housekeeper's warming pan);
the famous library went sky-high;
contemporary accounts refer to streams of books tossed
enormously by drafts of heat onto nearby mountains...

in 1810 Johnes rebuilt, including a Pleasure Dome
by John Nash as North Wing — being the very one S.T. Coleridge
saw and remembered later in Somerset one porlock-personed day...

in 1811, Marianne, the belovèd only child, died

in 1932, Chantrey's great monument in the Church near Hafod
was destroyed by fire, the firemen
foolishly hosing down the hot marble —

Johnes's head now lies to the right, at the base,
streaks of black and ochre quite covering it...

in 1958, the Forestry Commission dynamited Hafod as
"a menace to the Public Safety"

in 1966, there is a caravan site where Hafod, where
Eden stood...

from Kubla Khan
to Caravan

a stately,
measured

doom,

decreed…

hoo hoo
hee hee
say the locals!

—ஒ—

ALLEN BERESFORD, FARMER,
ON NOBILITY IN LANGSTROTHDALE CHASE

if thou piss free,
fart dry,
and pay 20 shillings in t' pound,

no man can touch thee!

A.L.B. (1917–1978)

he was
oald as the fells
street as an arske's arse
sharp as whins
whick as a lop
wild as winter thunner
nice as an otter

and his throat war middlen slippy
and he is deed as a steann

but not gone
but not gone

Old Cumbrian Dialect —
fells: *hills*
street: *straight*
arske: *an aquatic salamander or lizard, confused with* asp
whins: *gorse*
whick: *lively*
lop: *a bed flea*
middlen: *a fair amount*

UP DENT

sumbody spak i' next rumm, ghooast siled away

my owd lass thowt
shoo'd give 'em
a reight Yorkshire sissup

soa shoo bout some
liver an' a caufheart
an' a bit o' bacon

an' shoo smothered it
with oonions an' heearbs
o' one sooart or tother

an' when it come on th' table
it sent up sich a smell
'at one haufo' th' fowk i' th' street
had ther maaths watterin'

THE TRIUMPH OF CRAFT: A VIGNETTE FROM THE HEBRIDES FOR A HOME ARTS & INDUSTRIES EXHIBITION AS ARRANGED BY MARY FRAZER-TYTLER WATTS UNDER THE ELMS AT COMPTON, SURREY

lad asks Bessie
the old lady
in the factory

well then, what do you do
with all that steel wool
you steal?

well then,
I'm knittin'
a kettle

Mary Watts, the young second wife of G. F. Watts, painter and Honorary President of the Anti-Tight-Lacing Society (Gertie Tipple, Secretary), in her designs for the Watts Memorial Chapel at Compton, near Guilford, Surrey, created one of the unique fantasies in all of architecture: Celtic plus Art Nouveau plus Obsessive Theosophical... Watts, himself, needs revision on the basis of such paintings as The Sower of Systems, *where he comes out minor-league Gustave Moreau. And, after all, to quote the authoritative words of Violet A. Wlock, B.A., Deputy Curator of the Castle Museum, York, 1939–47, in her "A Chat on the Valentine": "...crinolines are creeping their way to fashion, there is even a whisper of tight lacing..."*

Sʳ YOU WRITT TO ME

about a good strong boy for the gardener

I have inquired one from the Boarders
which I am opinion
will doe very well

he
has been alwayes bred up with husbandry

he
is a good comely boy

he
is comed of very honnest parents

he
knows nothing of vice

the gardener
may make him as he pleases

his friends
will give him good country cloaths
and shirts and othre things

pray Sʳ
lett me know
if you have occasion
for him

ADUMBRATIONS OF MEPHITIC PHANTASMAGORIA
PRODUCED BY A ROADSIGN IN MILD & SUNNY
KIRKBY LONSDALE

raised manholes
for next mile

WORKS SIGN ON THE A-684
APPROACHING SEDBERGH THE BALEFUL

diversion
ends...

AUTUMN COMES TO THE
UPLANDS OF BRITAIN

it's quiet here and
the only sound you
hear is the occasional
thud as someone else
dies of extreme boredom

THE LAST WANK OF MAJOR WEDGWOOD-WANKER

old
china
hand

job

VII. THE FLOWER-HUNTER IN THE FIELDS

THE DECONSTRUCTIONIST GARDEN

me,

and the
weeds

PREVIOUSLY LOST LYRIC FRAGMENT
FROM THE PEN OF JOHANN PETER HEBEL,
"RUSTIC BARD OF THE BLACK FOREST"

Wenn Die Sonne untergeht
Denn Die Hosen von den Landtsknaben untergehen.

When the sun goes down,
that's when the farmboys' pants go down.

THE FLOWER-HUNTER IN THE FIELDS
for Agnes Arber

a flame azalea, mayapple, maple, thornapple
plantation

a white cloud in the eye
of a white horse

a field of bluets moving
below the black suit
of William Bartram

bluets, or "Quaker Ladies," or some say
"Innocence"

bluets and the blue of gentians and
Philadelphia blue laws!

high hills,

stone cold
sober

as October

---

*Bartram's name to the Seminole was "Puc-Puggy," the Flower-Hunter. He remains one of
the very few great men to have visited the Florida Lotophagi since Cabeza de Vaca…
I am most indebted to Mrs. Arber for the two books of hers I know:* Herbals *and* The
Mind and the Eye *(both Cambridge).* Herbals *and* The Mind and the Eye *(both
Cambridge).*

TWO PASTORALS FOR SAMUEL PALMER
AT SHOREHAM, KENT

I. *"If the Night Could Get Up & Walk"*

I cannot put my hand into
a cabbage to turn
on the light, but

the moon moves over
the field of dark cabbage and an
exchange fills
all veins.

The cabbage is also a globe
of light, the two globes

now two eyes in
my saturated

head!

II. *"One Must Try Behind the Hills"*

Eight Great Dahlias stood
beyond the Mountains.

They set fire to the Sun
in a black wood
beyond the Mountains,

in the Valley of Vision.

In the Valley of Vision

the Fission of
Flowers

yields all Power
in the Valley of Vision.

Eight Suns
on Eight Stems,

aflame!

Readers are referred to Geoffrey Grigson's two books: Samuel Palmer's Valley of Vision
(Phoenix House, London, 1960); and Samuel Palmer: The Visionary Years *(Routledge,
London, 1947). My titles are from letters by Palmer to George Raymond.*

THE DERACINATION

definition: root,

"a growing point,
an organ of absorption, an aerating organ,
a good reservoir, or
means of support"

Vernonia glauca, order Compositae,
"these tall perennials with
corymbose cymes of bright-purple heads of
tubular flowers
with conspicuous stigmas"

I do not know the Ironweed's root,
but I know it rules September

and where the flowers tower
in the wind there is a burr of
sound empyrean...the mind
glows and the wind drifts...

epiphanies pull up
from roots

epiphytic, making it up

out of the air

THE DISTANCES TO THE FRIEND

Thoreau,
grabbing on, hard,

a red, raw
muskrat ...

thought to eat it,
stifling all repulsion

so sat by the quagmire,
cranky, no cannibal, too
uninvolved
to get to man

so simply

we, the
heirs, hear other rustlings:

the grass stirs like an
androgyne,
the man

Based on an incident at Walden Pond, Massachusetts.

in our hearts stands
his fear
on its head,
savagely—

       inversed, nervelessly,
we sweat past each other,
unrelieved:

bitter landscapes,
         unlovely

TAOIST FORETASTE OF SPRINGTIME

busy as
a jaybird's ass

in mulberry
season!

A PILEATED WOODPECKER'S RESPONSE TO FOUR DOGWOOD BERRIES

(1) kuk

(2) kuk kuk

(3) kuk-kuk

(4) kukkuk

LE CONTE HIGH-TOP

under the rondelay
the sun

into the wind and rain a
winter wren

again, again —

its song
needling the pines

SPREADING CLEAR, PINK SPIKES (MOST SOILS)

Polygo-
num

bistorta

Super-

bum

METROPOLOPHIUM DIRHODUM

ants feed
from a honeydew
excreted from the anus of
the greenfly
and fight off
the predatory ladybirds as a
kind of quid
pro quo

COBWEBBERY

*...The spirit and the will survived, but something
in the soul perished.*
—D.H. Lawrence

the best spiders for soup
are the ones under
stones —

ask the man who is one:
plain white american

(not blue gentian red indian yellow sun black caribbean)

hard heart,
cold mind's found

a home
in the ground

"a rolling stone, *nolens volens,*
ladles no soup"

maw, rip them boards off
the side the house

and put the soup pot on

and plant us some petunias
in the carcass of the chevrolet

and let's stay here
and rot in the fields

and sit still

The Lawrence quote is from his introduction to Edward Dahlberg's first novel, Bottom Dogs *(City Lights, San Francisco, 1961). He spoke of the American character...* "nolens volens": *willy-nilly.*

THE GROUNDS

the Left Foot hit,
    deeply implanted,
        at the edge of the Garden,
and Garlic sprang up!

Legend is legion, engendering green in the groundwork we work
to prepare a Spring in ourselves; to air the sound
in ourselves

Belovèd Andrew Marvell, restore the furrows, and the elms
and melody!

Lusters stir the row! Poe's
Valley of the Many-Colored-Grass became
the Vale of Arnheim. Potomac's Valley shall become
a domain we create, an inchoate
scene where snows wane
and bulbs burn under the winter ground.

At the margins of thought, on the margins of the river, the winter
surrenders to the hosts of Great Venus.

By the fires of her campgrounds her hosts
sing her Vigil:

A poem for the prophetic Edward Dahlberg, who wrote me he felt "caught in the middle between the Marxists who I think have killed letters and the Cartels who have destroyed everything, the earth, the furrow, the elms, human affections, the liver, and I think the pudendum too..."

tomorrow shall be love to the lover,
and to the loveless too,
tomorrow shall be love!

We are where there is
a green ground —
                    and singing...

HEART-SONG DEAR TO THE AMERICAN PEOPLE

don't let the sun set on your head! I said
to the goldenrod

it stood
in the pine wood

out back
it was black

as a heart

ENTHUSIAST

literature — the way we ripen ourselves
by conversation, said
Edward Dahlberg...

we flower in talk, we slake
our thirsts in a brandy of heated speech, song
sweats through the pores,
trickles a swarm
into the sounding keyboard,

pollen falls
across the blackened paper...

always idle — before and
after
the act:

making meat
of vowels
in cells
with sticky feet

A VULNERARY
for Robert Duncan

one comes to language from afar, the ear
fears for its sound-barriers —

but one "comes"; the language "comes" for
The Beckoning Fair One

*plant you now, dig you
later,* the plaint stirs winter
earth...

air in a hornet's nest
over the water makes a
solid, six-sided music...

a few utterly quiet scenes, things
are very far away — *"form
is emptiness"*

comely, comely, love trembles

and the sweet-shrub

THE FAMILIARS
for Geoffrey Grigson

in the Appalachians
we plant a campion,

a "Rattlesnake-Master."

Master Thomas Campion,
plant your garden in our face,
turn all our thoughts to eyes,

> Where we such pleasing change doth view
> In every living thing,
> As if the world were born anew
> To gratify the spring.

O Starry Campion, *silene
stellata,*

laudamus te, benedicimus te ! ! !

—❧—

today is March twenty-first; the temperature sixty-one…

masses of rattlers as large as washtubs,
as large as watermelons,
lying in the sun by their dens.

the Indian said:
deer and ginseng and snake are allies
avenging each other;

but it is another, Spring Rain, god of rattlesnakes, puts
their signature
on the plantains by the ledge.

laudamus,
Crotalus horridus
horridus!

lead us
into the crevice into
the central den!

——◦●◦——

our insufflator, the warm sun,
warns us of the excrescences of language —

ecdysis, exuviation, desquamation —
it's the words that need to be shed.

so we coil on the stones with our blue eyes
calling for Mnemosyne to install
a new endothermal
control,

for the myth was: the shed skin was
immortal

(afflatus filling the skin
in the wind at night).

"the skinne that ye snake casts in ye spring tyme, being sod in wine,
is a remedie for ye paine in the eares"

    — Dioscorides

paeans in our ears!
Greek, Cherokee & United States of American Paeans,

that a caduceus of Viper's Bugloss
may cleanse our ears to hear —

even to the Language of the Birds!

for the Scripture is written:
"Plants at One End, Birds at the Other."

    ——◉◞——

This "bookish" poem is derived from a variety of reading: James Mooney's Myths of the
Cherokee *(Bureau of American Ethnology, Washington, 1900) and Laurence M.
Klauber's incredible* Rattlesnakes *(2 volumes: University of California Press, Berkeley and
Los Angeles, 1956) are the principal sources... From Thomas Campion, I have made several
paraphrases and quoted, almost verbatim, a stanza from* Number XII *of the* Second
Book of Airs... *The "Gloria" I have in mind is that of Francis Poulenc... The quote from
Dioscorides is from* The Greek Herbal *(Hafner, New York, 1959)... "Plants at One End,
Birds at the Other"—from Saurat's* Gods of the People. *He heard this in Hyde*

houseleek & garlic,
hyssop & mouse;

hawk & hepatica,
hyacinth, finch!

crawl, all
exits

from
hibernaculum!

*Park, London… "The Familiars," being dedicated to Mr. Grigson, offers small thanks
indeed for his extraordinary* The Englishman's Flora *(Phoenix House, London, 1955) and
for his wide-ranging work as a whole… Lest I give the impression that these little poems are
manufactured strictly from other literature, let me say that their spirit and ecology derive
from a summer's hike of 1,457 miles along the Appalachian Trail — Georgia to New York at
the Hudson River at Bear Mountain, 1961. Since walking is one thing and writing anoth-
er, men's minds are better nourishment for poems than raisins are.*

VIII. HOMAGES, ELEGIES & VALEDICTIONS

O FOR A MUSE OF FIRE!

Date: Tuesday, May 13, 1958 —
a date previously memorable in history for the birth of
Joe Lewis (1914),
the Empress Maria Theresa (1717),
and the beheading of
Johan Van Olden Barnveldt (1619)

Place: Wrigley Field, Chicago, Illinois

Time: 3:06 p.m.; warm and sunny; breeze steady, right to left

Attendance: 5,692 (paid)

Situation: top of the sixth; Cardinals trailing the Cubs, 3–1: one out;
Gene Green on second

Public Address: "Batting for Jones, #6, Stan Musial!"

The Muse muscles up; Stan the Man stands in...and
O, Hosanna, Hosanna, Ozanna's boy, Moe Drabowsky comes in

2 and 2
"a curve ball, outside corner, higher
than intended —
I figured he'd hit it in the ground"

(*"it felt fine!"*)

a line shot to left, down the line,
rolling deep for a double…

(*"it felt fine!"*)

Say, Stan, baby, how's it feel to hit 3,000?

"Ugh, it feels fine"

---

*Only six major-league players in baseball history had hit safely 3,000 times prior to this
occasion. The density of the information surrounding the event continues to surprise me
and rather belies Tocqueville's assertion that Americans cannot concentrate.*

DANGEROUS CALAMUS EMOTIONS

"Walt Whitman is in town —
I have just seen him, but
publicly of course."

                traffic jam! tram drivers,
                    streetcar conductors,
                    Sergeant Tom Sawyer, Peter
                    Doyle, all

                the Camerados & Lovers

            DO NOT TALK TO DRIVER
            WHILE BUS IS IN MOTION, do not motion
            to driver, or
            bus will talk; walk, do not run
            to the nearest; and do not buss
            bus drivers!

deliver us, deliver ass
from puritan transit!

W.C.W.: "him and that Jesuit, them with the variable feet —
        they changed it!"

variable, viable,
veritable Walt

Whitman!

---

*The initial quotation is from the sedulous Mr. Emerson to the prissy Mrs. Emerson, one of
the New England gentry who did not approve of Whitman's athletic, amative, democratic
tastes... Dr. Williams is referring to Whitman and Gerard Manley Hopkins — for him the
founders of the modern poem.*

THE ADHESIVE AUTOPSY OF WALT WHITMAN, 1892

"Gentlemen, look on this wonder…
and wonders within there yet":

"pleurisy of the left side, consumption
of the right lung,

general miliary tuberculosis
and parenchymatous nephritis…a fatty

liver a huge stone
filling the gall,

a cyst in the adrenal, tubercular abscesses
involving the bones,

and pachymeningitis"

"that he was a Kosmos is a piece of news we were
hardly prepared for…"

good bie Walter dear

The quotations are, verbatim, from the Philadelphia and Camden newspapers…the farewell is by Whitman's mother, who could not spell properly.

A VALEDICTION FOR MY FATHER (1898–1974)

all the old things
are gone now

and the people are
different

AN ORNAMENT FOR DICK NICKEL, BURIED IN THE DEMOLITION OF SULLIVAN'S STOCK EXCHANGE, CHICAGO

a flower appears
amid the leaves of
its parent plant

EDWARD DAHLBERG

Hostility, Rancor,
Spleen, a Foe —

what else is my guerdon
in this flensed world?

COMPANIONS FOR THE DARK SLATE HEADSTONE OF CHARLES JOHN OLSON JR.

small,
yellow

flower
heads

of
tansy

Tansy,
fr. Gr. *athanasia*
(deathlessness)

because of
the characteristic
permanent possession
it takes of
the soil

he takes of
the soul

TO CHARLES OSCAR

may there be stiff reeds
for your hands
among the asphodels,
Charles

and wind
to move them
over the bronze water
onto paper

and Lethe for us,
left
with your shattered
inkstone

The painter Charles Oscar was murdered in New York City in 1961.

PASO DOBLE CALLED "SOMETHING" FOR PAUL BLACKBURN

something about
being six foot four
not
five foot two

something
about those very delicate wrists
how I never felt able to hold them

or really look him in the eyes
like I wanted to

those years before Levi's
and cowboy hats
and That Old (Macho) Gang o' Mine,
and all thatthere,

buddy boy

THE PHOTOGRAPHER LOOKS AT HIS PRINTS
AND TURNS POET
for Ralph Eugene Meatyard, 1925–1972

this picture for
instance
of Lucybelle with Wendell Berry
on his farm

he raised a small crop of peanuts
which is there
in its entirety

the shadows
are my contribution
to the construction
of the picture

—◦∾—

I find
a background

and put
content

in front
of it

—◦∾—

the rear
of the truck

swing-ropes coming down
branch coming across

shadows on the side
of Lucybelle

there's got
to be more in a picture

than the billboard sight
we first
get

of it

———◦ఞ◦———

in the doctor's office
the other day

people had lines running on their jawline
where the mask-line would come

if they were 70 years old
instead of 40 years old

———◦ఞ◦———

how demure some
people can look

how frightened how
pleased

all this that & the other
all become

of importance

—⚬—

hard time
getting this little boy
to wear the mask

looks as if
he was having a hard time
doing it

—⚬—

the hands
on this man

on the play-toy they're
sitting on

—⚬—

how Lucybelle
raises
her eyebrows

sometimes

—⚬—

the toes
of this little girl

the important part
of this
particular picture

—⊙—

it could be you

or you or
you

you know there's a person
back there

you have no idea in the world
who

add a little mask

ON COWEE RIDGE
December 13, 1993

John Gordon Boyd
died on the birthday
of three remarkable, and remarkably different, writers:
Heinrich Heine, Kenneth Patchen, Ross MacDonald

John, too, was just as remarkable, blessed with an inherent "graciousness"
and with extraordinary eyes & ears...

I think of two texts
on the grievous occasion of his death:

"Religion does not help me.
   The faith that others give to what is unseen,
   I give to what I can touch, and look at.
   My Gods dwell in temples
   made with hands."
      — Oscar Wilde, in *De Profundis*

and two lines of Rainer Maria Rilke,
John's favorite poet,
that say it all...

Was tun Sie, Gott,
Wenn ich bin stürbe?

"What will you do,
   God, when I am dead?"

REFLECTIONS FROM *APPALACHIA*

dawn songs in the dews of young orange trees;
and ranging orisons; and wordless longings

sung in tranquillity's waters sliding in sun's
light;

and benisons sung in these trees…

in these, yes, it is the "ah-ness," yes, it is the course of adrenaline,
but, it is the lens opening of Frederick Delius's luminous blind eye:
f-stop open —
all things measureless lucidities,

my eyes
so in tune: atonement, at-one-ment is
atonement,

what is meant by not
being able to focus two eyes…

they lie on the horizon,
they lie on the great St. Johns River's waters
in the monocular sunlight

three miles wide
lid to lid

STILL WATER FOR LORINE NIEDECKER (1903–1970)

she seined words
as others stars
or carp

laconic as
a pebble
in the Rock River

along the bank
where the peony flowers
fall

her tall friend
the pine tree
is still there

to see

ELEGY FOR A PHOTOGRAPH
OF WILLIAM CARLOS WILLIAMS

the last, absolutely the Last
Dahlia

on Ridge Road, Rutherford, New Jersey, October 18, 1960 —

you have outlived It,
and wear the Epaulet
to prove it...

I salute you in your
Garden State!

You taught us to
scrape all the Leaves off the Bottom of the Barrel,
because the Leaves can equal

the Sacred Red Anemones of Osiris
falling in the Blue Waterfalls of
Lebanon —

and you knew it

IN MARSDEN HARTLEY'S HAND

happily contented
to be climbing the heights and the clouds
by the brush method

— ❧ —

they
have to
come of
themselves

— ❧ —

place me in the middle
between these lovers of mine
and there you have us

— ❧ —

golden-glories
of my heart's gate

— ❧ —

I see
the mail carrier
coming down
the field

— ❧ —

I know
what I see

—⚬—

to walk on
throughout the exquisite days
with you

enough that you
call me brother,
friend, lover

a kiss
to you
across
these
isolated hills

—⚬—

one can't have all
things in the hills

yet I found your letter
here in the hills

—⚬—

better
to be walking about
with new young stars
in one's hand
than fumbling over
old meteors

—⚬—

a big broad shoulder
to brush by...

the flicker
of the yellow butterfly...

—⚬—

somehow
this business of one
isn't big enough

—⚬—

love again,
always love

MARSALA & WATER FOR EDWARD LEAR

old, ill-tempered, and queer,
he wept
on the top of
a weir:

"the castor bean
and five-day cricket paté
was trop catastrophique

comme la vie,
c'est beeeeeeeeeeeeeeeeeeeeeeeeeeeeeeeeeeeeeeeeeeeeeeeeeeestly!

...so where is Gatto Foss, when at this moment
I'm about to become catsmeat under the dotty Ligurian skies?"

Foss is about to leave Paradise
with his new group, MIGHTY CAT AND THE CATAMITES,
in eight Lear jets
(you can already hear these dizzies
caterwauling like the lads in Holman Hunt's painting
May Morning on Magdalen Tower)

those are some guys, Edward,
they read your stuff in the nursery,
they have the odd chuckle,
they'd no more kiss you or hold you
than your famous friend, Chichester Fortescue —

you'd better forget it...

ave-
nue

atque

volley-
ball!

WHO IS LITTLE ENIS?

LITTLE ENIS is
"one hunnert an' 80 lbs of
dynamite
with a 9-inch
fuse"

his real name is
Carlos Toadvine
which his wife Irma Jean
pronounces *Carlus*

Carlos says
Toadaveenie is a eyetalyun name,
used to be lots of 'em
round these parts

Ed McClanahan is the World's Leading Little Enis Freak
and all this information comes to you from a weekend in Winston
with Big Ed telling the lore of Lexington, Kentucky,
which is where Enis has been hanging it out for years and years,
at Boots Bar and Giuseppe's Villa and, now, The Embers,
pickin' and singin' rockabilly style

Carlus ain't what he was
according to Irma Jean's accounts
(and even to his own):

he was sittin' there one night in the kitchen at home
tellin' stories and talkin' trash about Irma Jean —
with her right there with her hair put up in them pink plastic curlers —
about how these days he likes to pop it to her dog-style
just now and again and how she
likes it pretty damn well
when they wander all over the house
and end up in the living-room corner —
"I'm just afraid Carlus will run us out of the door and down the street
opposite the automatic laundry…"

The 9-inch fuse hung down Enis's left leg
is called, familiarly,
Ol' Blue

Ol' Blue used to be in the pink! —
way in…

Blue has a head on him like a tomcat
and ribs like a hongry hound

and he used to get so hard
a cat
couldn't
scratch it…

but now that Enis has the cirrhosis
and takes all thesehyar harmones
Ol' Blue just don't
stand up
like a little man
and cut no mustard
anymore

But Enis will smile and say
let's all have a drink, maybe I can drown thatthere liver of ours,
it's no bigger'n a dime nohow anymore, it just floats in there...

Hey, Blue, let's shake that thang!
Turn a-loose this oldie
by my boy Elvis —
a golden oldie!
let's go, Blue!

And off they go
into the Wild Blue
Yonder in the Blue
Grass...

Carlos & Blue,
thinking of you...

Hail & Farewell!

DIZZY AT THE FROG

the legendary
yes ladies &
gentlemen
the legendary
John Birks Gillespie
tells how he's
related to Rameses the Groovy
who ran this groovy place
called Cush

on the Nile
in about twelve hundred B.C.

and shit
it was some sort
of civilization
oh my

yes so he's composed
"Cush"
to know where his ancestor's head was
at, no

and so dizzy it is
to start watching those
pouches on either side his eyes
as he blows those
choruses in "Cush"

say, man,
are those
monkey nuts,
or chocolate
tomatoes?

they are
somethin' else!

they belong on
Mr. Peanut

as he struts
in Paradise...

TEXTS FOR THE BILLIE HOLIDAY MEMORIAL SCULPTURE BY TYLDEN STREETT IN A PARK OFF EUTAW PLACE, BALTIMORE, MARYLAND

when I sing them I
live them again
and I love them

———❧———

without feeling,
whatever you do
amounts to nothing

———❧———

maybe I'm proud enough
to want to remember
Baltimore

———❧———

when you sing it
other people can feel
something too

———❧———

I never hurt anybody
but myself
and that's nobody's business
but my own

———❧———

there had to be
some good
in everybody

———❧———

you have to laugh
or cry
all alone

BROTHER ANTONINUS

he retired in 1982
to a rustic cabin
he named kingfisher flat

he told his class
this is not an
introduction to poetry but
an introduction to yourselves

"THE ENCHANTED BATH-SPONGE"

Bucky Fuller says, Fella,
if you don't think it's poetry,
call it "ventilated prose"

Please, if they don't see trees,
please let them see
these "enchanted bath-sponges"
        — manic plea, courtesy John Cotman

his space over the water
fills with the noise of birds catching
flies, but the watercolour paper is
completely silent

lines as
lines, spaces
as
spaces

pleasures as
what they
are

I get tired of readers who know everything —
that's *all* they know!

A MATHOM FOR J.R.R. TOLKIEN

on the streams of Westernesse outside the Shire
the Pipe-Weed grows with the Golden-Seal...

do not forget this in your zeal:
the emperies of elves *and* men are flowers!

shun Ranunculus at Raven Knob,
and Black Cohosh and Columbine
and Rue-Anemone —

the human minions/
the elven votaries!

beware the Hellebore
on Rabun Bald, or Barad-dûr, or Erebor!

A "mathom," as defined in the Hobbit-lore of The Lord of the Rings *(3 volumes: George Allen & Unwin Ltd, London, 1954), is something for which there is no immediate use, but which one is unwilling to throw away... The plants invoked are all members of the family Ranunculaceae (Crowfoot) to complement Raven Knob. The latter is in Rabun County, Georgia, as is Rabun Bald, third-highest mountain in the state. Barad-dûr is the Dark Tower of Mordor; Erebor is the Lonely Mountain of Dale... I take the opportunity to reaffirm that Professor Tolkien's trilogy is the most magical work of the age. I began reading him at age 8 — even that wasn't soon enough.*

FURNITURE MUSIC: "THREE-PIECE SUITE IN THE SHAPE OF A PORRIDGE"

we feel ourselves among
Poets when entering
the rooms of Mackintosh
says *Deutsche Kunst*

chocolate éclair
chairs for fairies
declares Glasgow
laird

it often seems
as if the dream
were a personal aim
says *Deutsche Kunst*

la chair est triste
hissed Red-Hair
MacLank Shanks

O form divine, O attic, scotch-shaped
divanpoetical davenpoet! —

settee, set-to

OH, OUR RONALD

his voice as
due
to talking to
so few
people

Mr.
Fir-
bank
"ab-
sorbed

a
single

grape"

FRANCIS BACON

a delicate, lively, hazel Eie...

Dr. Harvey tolde me
it was like the Eie
of a viper

ALLAH MAHNYHERDHA

Arcangelo Corelli, Seen in Concise Concert with Coventina,
Nymph of the Tyne, and One of Her Minions, by GFH

he was very simple and
unpretentious
in all
his habits

would on no account
hire a carriage
but went
on foot

says Handel

"Si suona a Napoli!"

"Aye, they can sing 'em
at Wylam!"

says Handel

Antonio Vivaldi, il Preto Rosso, Writes from Venice

anything
that I can do

that is worthwhile

I do at home
at my desk

P.S.: last year's music
does not pay any more

the famous Sassone (Handel the Saxon)
is the lion
nowadays

Alessandro on His Son, Domenico Scarlatti, & His Sonatas Modernas

his talent found scope indeed,
but it was not the sort of talent for that place...

I send him away
from Rome also,
since Rome
has no roof to shelter music
that lives here
in beggary...

if his own playing were admired,
he would turn the conversation on Handel,
crossing himself at the same time

Fryderyk Franciszek Chopin

(Also Born on 1 March)
Quotes for Basil Bunting from *The Musical World,*
An English Newspaper of His Own Day:

"his admirers regard him
as a species of musical Wordsworth,
inasmuch as
he scorns popularity
and writes entirely up to
has own standard of excellence..."

Quel remplissage piquant!
no organ of consistency…
no bump of epicism…

Sir Edward Elgar Sends a Telegram from the Malverns:

JOLLY GOOD STUFF!

(CHUFF CHUFF)

ONE TUNE LIKE

THAT'S

ENOUGH

IN LIFE

THE WRECK ON THE A-222 IN RAVENSBOURNE VALLEY

There are more things to love
than we would dare to hope for.
—Richard of St. Victor

where the car hit him, fireweed sprang with
blazons of fennel

and umbels
of dill fell
through the spokes of a wheel

on Whitsun holiday to the sun, Denton
Welch spun a web in his crushed cycle,

sat in the seat, spine curled up like a spider—

and spied: "saw
           the very drops of sweat glittering frostily
           between the shoulder blades"

           of a lad

...on and on he spied and bled from the blades of his cycle,
small as a spider,
hiding in the fireweed, getting
wet from the skins of many human suns aground
at the Kentish river near
Tunbridge Wells,

where the dill
lulls,

and all boys
spoil...

The dire chronicle of Denton Welch's (1917–1948) accident and illness is told in A Voice Through a Cloud, *originally published by John Lehmann in Great Britain, republished in America by the University of Texas Press.*

AN OMEN FOR STEVIE SMITH

*"Being alive is like being
in enemy territory."*

this is your aunt, Stevie,
and oh you must hurry!

The Man in Black
who waits tonight along the Lyke Wake Walk
has a gown for you
the colour of rowan berries;

a gown borne in air by hornets,
hagworms, and ants, riding
the backs of great bustards and herons…

your cats,
Brown and Fry and Hyde,
yes, Stevie, they too
shall come at last
to Whinny-Moor…

the five of you
shall dance that heath
to Death!

A FINAL WHIFF OF THE YORKSHIRE MOORS
FOR FRED DELIUS

"You needn't ask me to listen
to the Music of the Immortals."

an afternoon on
Ilkley Moor,
when the sun shone a long red light on the Swastika Stone, then
set behind Skipton,

tchuck tchick
tchuck tchick

Turdus delianus,
a new kind of thrush,
ceased its hopping
and cocked its head to one side
to hear the song soughing in the heather

tchuck tchick
tchuck tchick

in the dark
it became a boy called Fred again
and went home
to eat parkin

pee-wit cour-li cuckoo
pee-wit croo-ee cuckoo

"birds would sing
for him
whenever
he wanted them
to"

—☙—

tchuck tchick
tchuck tchick

a thrush brought
the ling
for your grave

from Baildon Moor

DIRGE FOR SEER-SCRIVENER, PRINCE-PLANGENT OF GORMENGHAST

"And the days move on
and the names of the months change
and the four seasons bury one another
and the field-mice draw upon their granaries"

—this is the kind of vision
Mervyn Peake shares with William Blake:

seeing
not with
but *thru*
the eye!

you get it, very very steady
in the *Titus* trilogy—

one extraordinary instance being
that passage in Book One, pp. 116–17,
where Steerpike spies the dead tree
high on the cyclopean walls
of Gormenghast Castle;

and in Book Two, Chapter Fifty-one, Section v:

"...A loosened stone falls from a high tower.
  A fly drops lifeless from a broken pane.
  A sparrow twitters in a cave of ivy..."

I can do nothing but quote
this fantastic man, like Kenneth Patchen,
creator of one Dark Kingdom,
unstrung by a darker one...

I lament all ravens and the owls in Hell
who stay his hand
and dis-connect this sun

---

*Mervyn Peake (1911–November 17, 1968, at Burcot, Oxfordshire) was perhaps the last
master of gothic delineation and the grotesque, though his prose comes from Melville and
Dickens and not Mrs. Radcliffe. Because of his disabling psychic illnesses we had no succes-
sors to the* Gormenghast Trilogy *or to such illustrations as those to the "Ancient Mariner"
or to* Alice in Wonderland. *Like Delius, Poe, Lovecraft, Coleridge, his time was no place
for him.*

MY QUAKER-ATHEIST FRIEND,
WHO HAS COME TO THIS MEETINGHOUSE SINCE 1913,
SMOKES & LOOKS OUT OVER THE RAWTHEY
TO HOLME FELL

what do you do
anything for?

you do it
for what the mediaevals would call
something like
the *Glory of God*

doing it for money,
that doesn't do it;

doing it for vanity,
that doesn't do it;

doing it to justify a disorderly life,
that doesn't do it

look at Briggflatts here...

it represents the best
that the people were able to do

they didn't do it for gain;
in fact, they must have
taken a loss

whether it is a stone next to a stone
or a word next to a word,
it is the *glory* —
the simple craft of it

and money and sex aren't worth
bugger-all, not
bugger-all

solid, common, *vulgar* words

the ones you can touch,
the ones that yield

and a respect for the music...

what else can you tell 'em?

ABOUT THE AUTHOR

JW was born in Asheville, North Carolina, in 1929. He was educated at St. Albans School, Princeton University, Atelier 17, the Institute of Design (Chicago), and Black Mountain College. His mentors include John Claiborne Davis, Aaron Siskind, Charles Olson, Lou Harrison, Paul Goodman, Kenneth Patchen, Kenneth Rexroth, Edward Dahlberg, Stefan Wolpe, Robert Duncan, Geoffrey Grigson, Basil Bunting, Ian Hamilton Finlay, Clarence John Laughlin, and Raymond Moore.

He has directed The Jargon Society, a writer's press devoted to poetry and photography, for fifty-four years. Some of its authors being Charles Olson, Robert Creeley, Russell Edson, Denise Levertov, Doris Ulmann, Paul Metcalf, Ronald Johnson, Alfred Starr Hamilton, Art Sinsabaugh, Ralph Eugene Meatyard, Lyle Bongé, Elizabeth Matheson, John Menapace, David Spear, Mina Loy, Lorine Niedecker, Bill Antony, Thomas A. Clark, Thomas Meyer, and Simon Cutts.

Mr. Williams has been a poet, publisher, essayist, book designer, photographer, and hiker of many long distances. The peripatetic life has taught him most of what he knows. Peripheral neuropathy has slowed him down a bit (too damn much hiking) — but, what the hell.

He has been around long enough to have heard John Philip Sousa (as a baby), Fritz Kreisler, Jascha Heifetz, Rachmaninoff, Horowitz, Flagstad, and Mae West. He's watched Sammy Baugh, Lou Gehrig, Bob Feller, DiMaggio, Jackie Robinson, and Willie Mays play. He's met Stieglitz, Steichen, Alvin Langdon Coburn, Imogen Cunningham, and Edward Weston; John Marin, Hans Arp, Hans Hofmann, Karl Knaths, Pevsner, Tchelitchew, Dalí. But Rupert Hart-Davis, the distinguished London publisher, told him: "After age 65 it is very important never to meet new people."

He divides his year between Skywinding Farm near Highlands, North Carolina, and Corn Close, a seventeenth-century stone cottage in Dentdale, Cumbria, England. He shares his life with Thomas Meyer, poet, astrologer, and translator. And a male marmalade cat named H-B Kitty, whose slaves they have become. Not a bad thing. They lead an aesthetic, monastic life in the tall weeds — not a bad thing, either. *The Literary Life* is far away. That's good, too.

The Chinese character for poetry is made up of two parts: "word" and "temple." It also serves as pressmark for Copper Canyon Press.

Founded in 1972, Copper Canyon Press remains dedicated to publishing poetry exclusively, from Nobel laureates to new and emerging authors. The Press thrives with the generous patronage of readers, writers, booksellers, librarians, teachers, students, and funders — everyone who shares the conviction that poetry invigorates the language and sharpens our appreciation of the world.

MAJOR FUNDING HAS BEEN PROVIDED BY:

The Paul G. Allen Family Foundation

Lannan Foundation

National Endowment for the Arts

The Starbucks Foundation

Washington State Arts Commission

For information and catalogs:
COPPER CANYON PRESS
Post Office Box 271
Port Townsend, Washington 98368
360-385-4925
www.coppercanyonpress.org

The text of this book is set in two faces designed by Matthew Carter: the Carter & Cone digitization of ITC Galliard, and Mantinia. Galliard is based on the designs of the Parisian punchcutter and typefounder Robert Granjon (1513–1590) and was originally released by Mergenthaler Linotype in 1978. Mantinia, released in 1993, and designed as a display face for Galliard, was inspired by and dedicated to Andrea Mantegna, one of the great artists of fifteenth century Italy, who painted and engraved the Roman epigraphic lettering of ancient monuments.

Design and composition by Jonathan Greene.

Printing and binding by McNaughton and Gunn, Inc.